The
SURVIVOR
TRIVIA
Game Book

*Note: This book was updated in 2024,
and contains questions that refer to records
set through Season 46 of "Survivor."*

What you need

- This book!
- 2-6 players
- A smartphone timer or stopwatch
- Scoring method (Pen and paper, or smartphone)

How to play

Choose a person to keep score.

General trivia questions are worth 1, 2 or 3 points based on difficulty. Although "Survivor" contestant last names are included in this book, players only need to provide the first name for a correct answer, unless otherwise noted.

The youngest player reads the first question to the player directly to his or her right. If the player answers correctly, he or she earns the number of points for that question. (Correct answers can be found on the page that follows each question.) The youngest player passes the book to the person on his or her left, who then asks the next question to the youngest player. Continue moving the book around your group in this fashion.

If only two players, simply pass the book back and forth.

If a player lands on a bonus round page, that person will have an opportunity to earn up to 8 points. Some of these questions involve a time limit. Read all instructions aloud when landing on a bonus round page, and use a timer when necessary. The question reader should keep track of correct answers in a bonus round, and tally the points for the scorekeeper.

The player with the most points at the end wins. You may choose to play the entire book. For a shorter round, elect to end the game on page 50 or page 100, and pick up from there next time.

Question

Who was the first ever
Survivor to find a hidden
immunity idol?

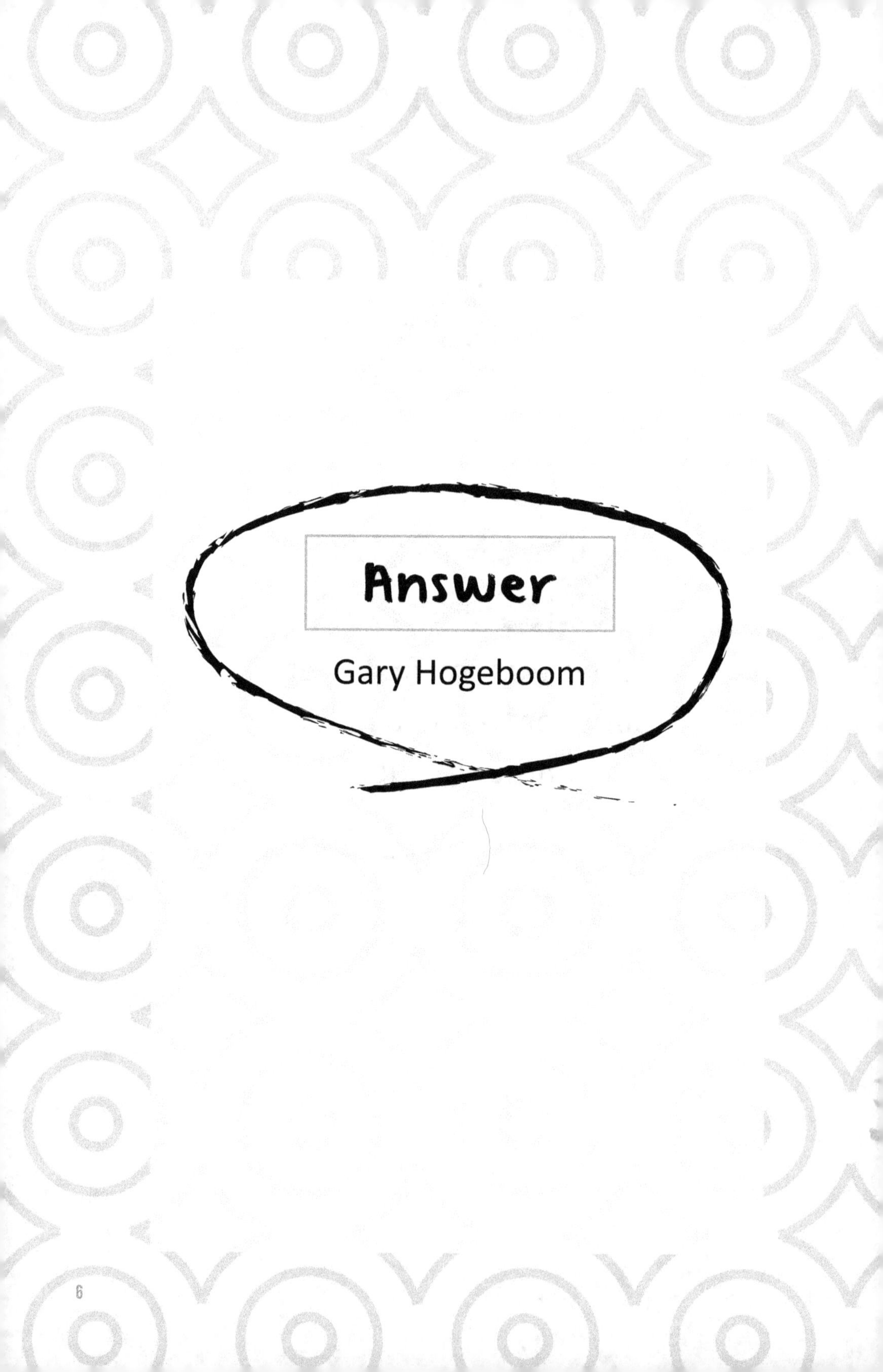
Answer
Gary Hogeboom

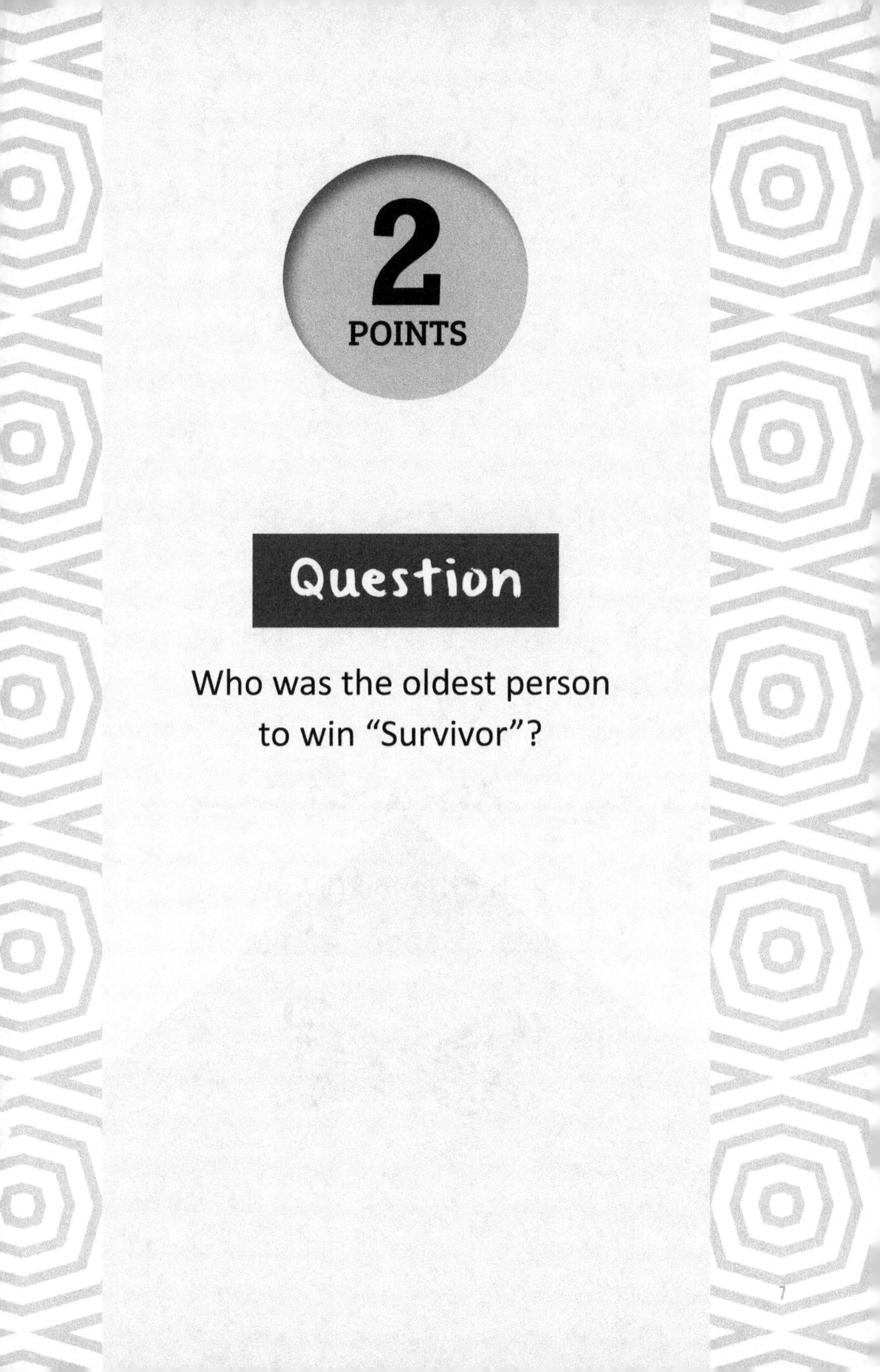

Question

Who was the oldest person
to win "Survivor"?

Answer

Bob Crowley (Won
"Survivor: Gabon" at age 57)

In what year did "Survivor" premiere?

2000

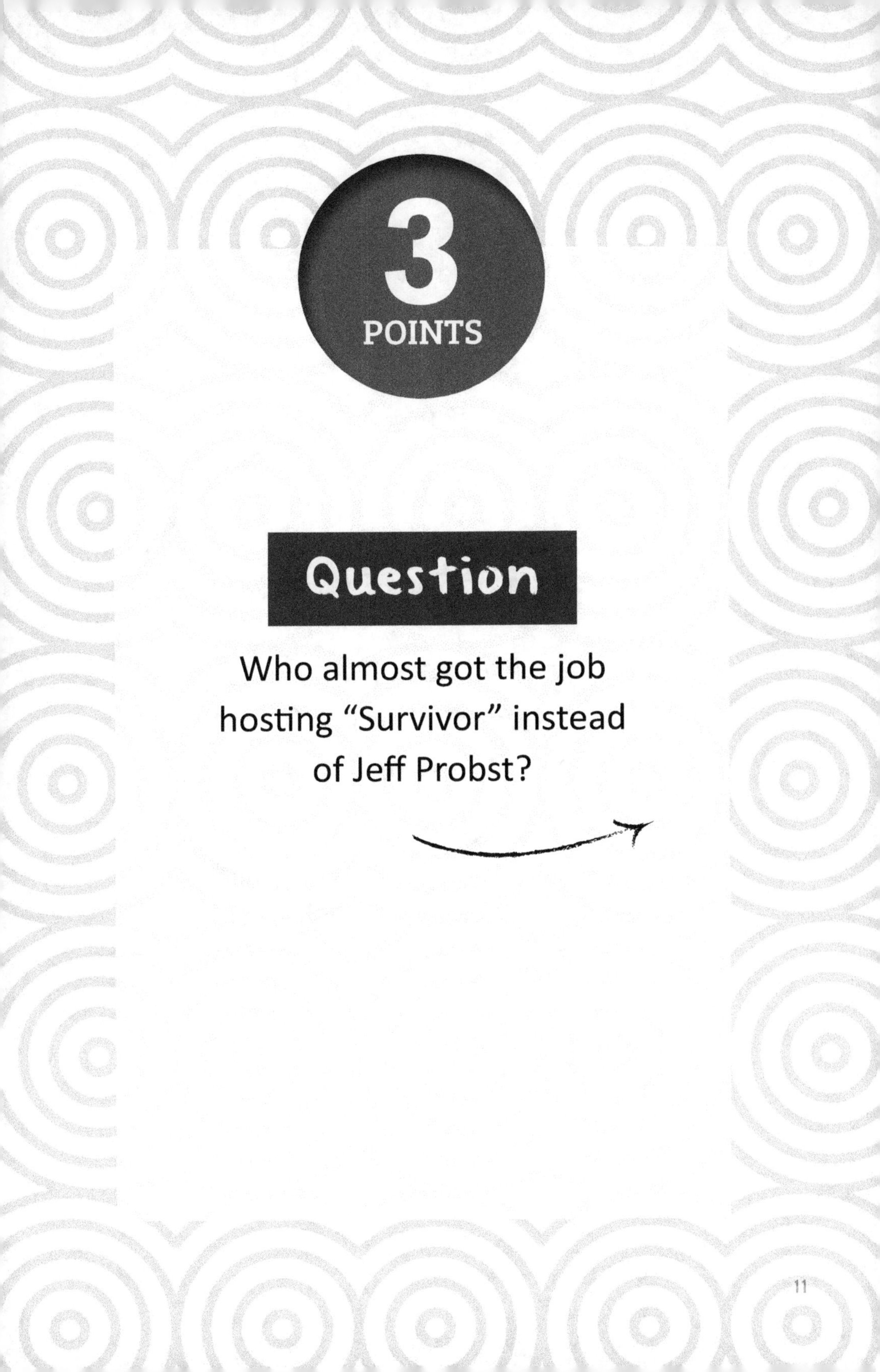

Question

Who almost got the job
hosting "Survivor" instead
of Jeff Probst?

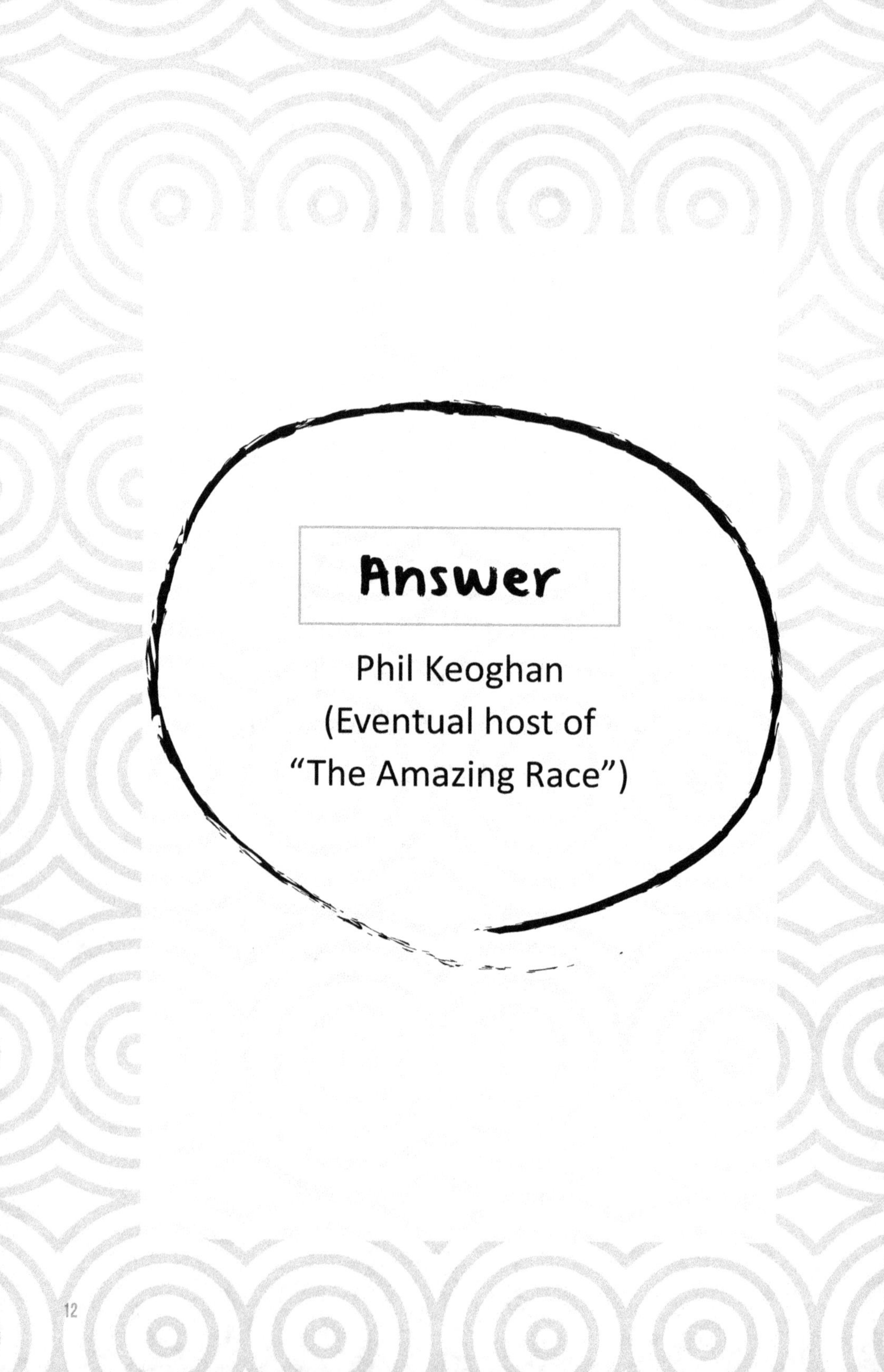

Answer

Phil Keoghan
(Eventual host of
"The Amazing Race")

BONUS
Round!

(No pressure or anything.)

BONUS Round!

You have 60 seconds to answer once the question is read aloud.
Through 46 seasons, 6 people whose first names start with the
letter T have won the game of "Survivor." Name them.
(One point for each name for a maximum of 6 points.)

Tina Wesson	Season 2, The Australian Outback
Tom Westman	Season 10, Palau
Todd Herzog	Season 15, China
Tyson Apostol	Season 27, Blood vs. Water
Tony Vlachos	Season 28, Cagayan; Season 40: Winners at War
Tommy Sheehan	Season 39, Island of the Idols

Question

Who was the first "Survivor" contestant to win the game twice?

Answer

Sandra Diaz-Twine

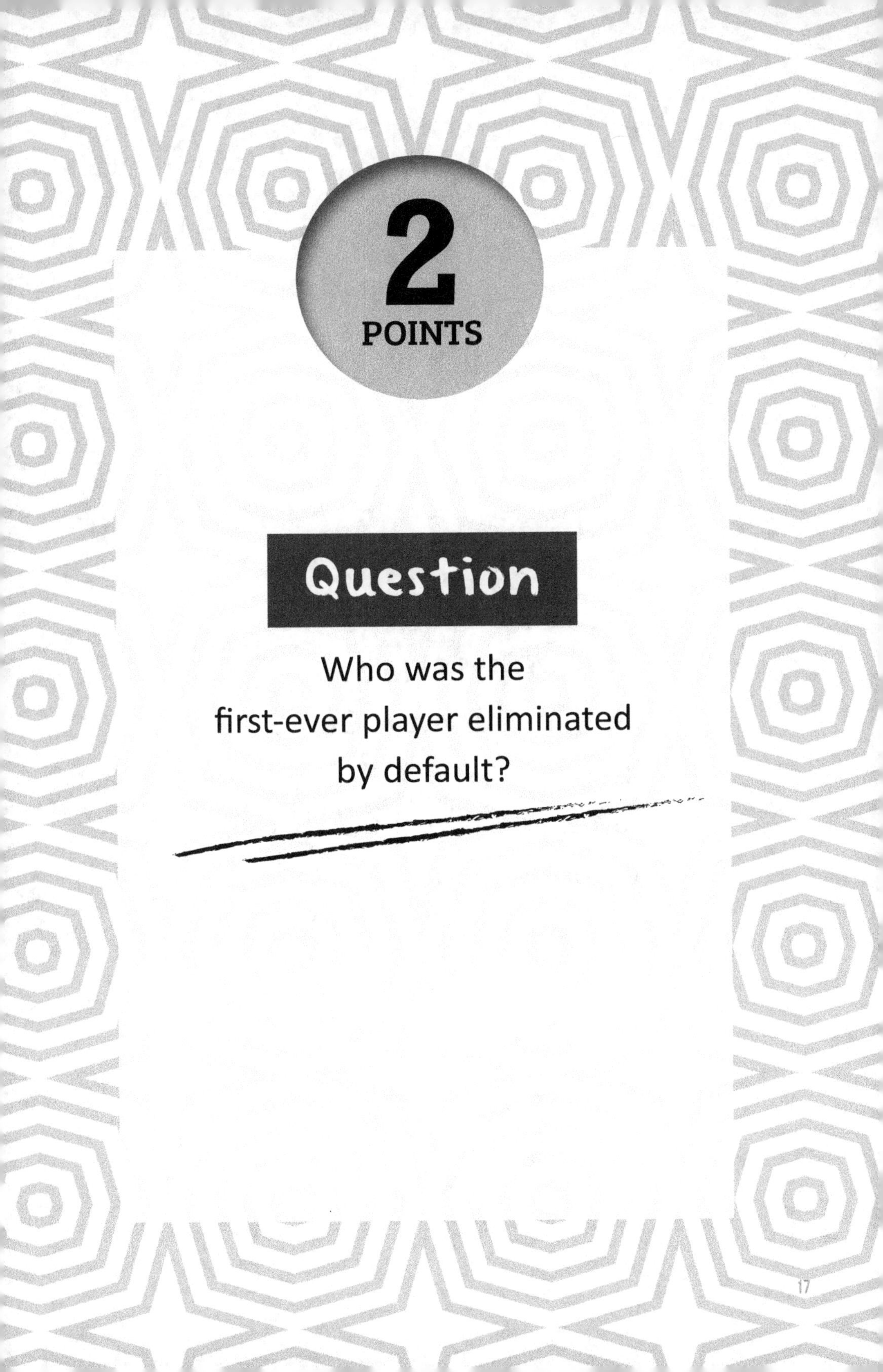

Question

Who was the
first-ever player eliminated
by default?

Answer

Cirie Fields
(In "Survivor: Game
Changers," she was voted out
after she was the only one
without an immunity idol at
Tribal Council.)

Question

Which Survivor agreed
to vote out her own mother
in the first "Survivor:
Blood vs. Water" season?

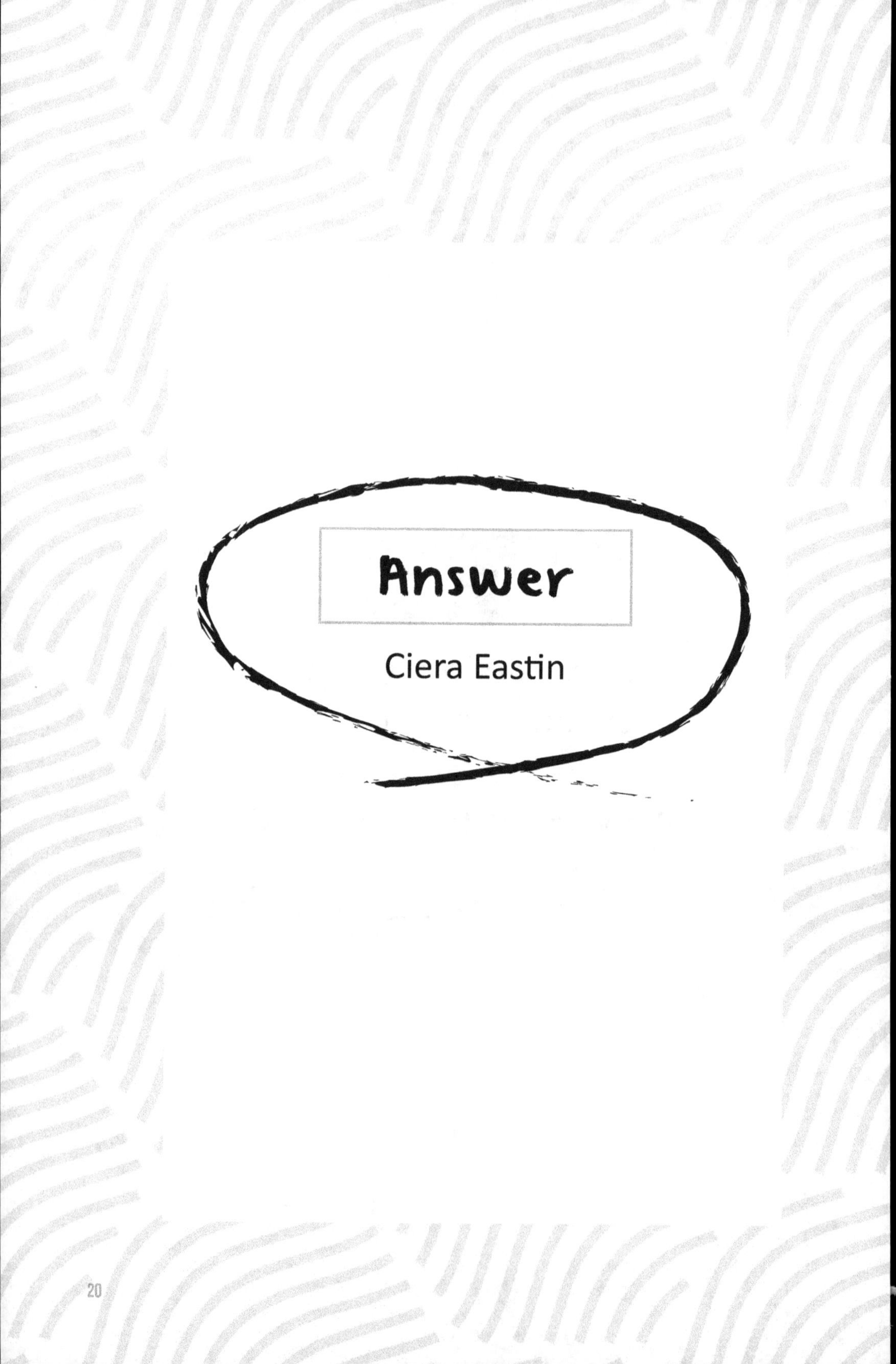
Answer
Ciera Eastin

Question

Which season 2 castaway removed coral from the Great Barrier Reef, a crime resulting in a fine?

Answer

Colby Donaldson

Who won "Survivor: Marquesas" and later said, "Survivor changed my life very little. I still shop at Walmart."

Answer

Vecepia Towery

Question

What castaway tricked his tribe into thinking his grandmother had just died?

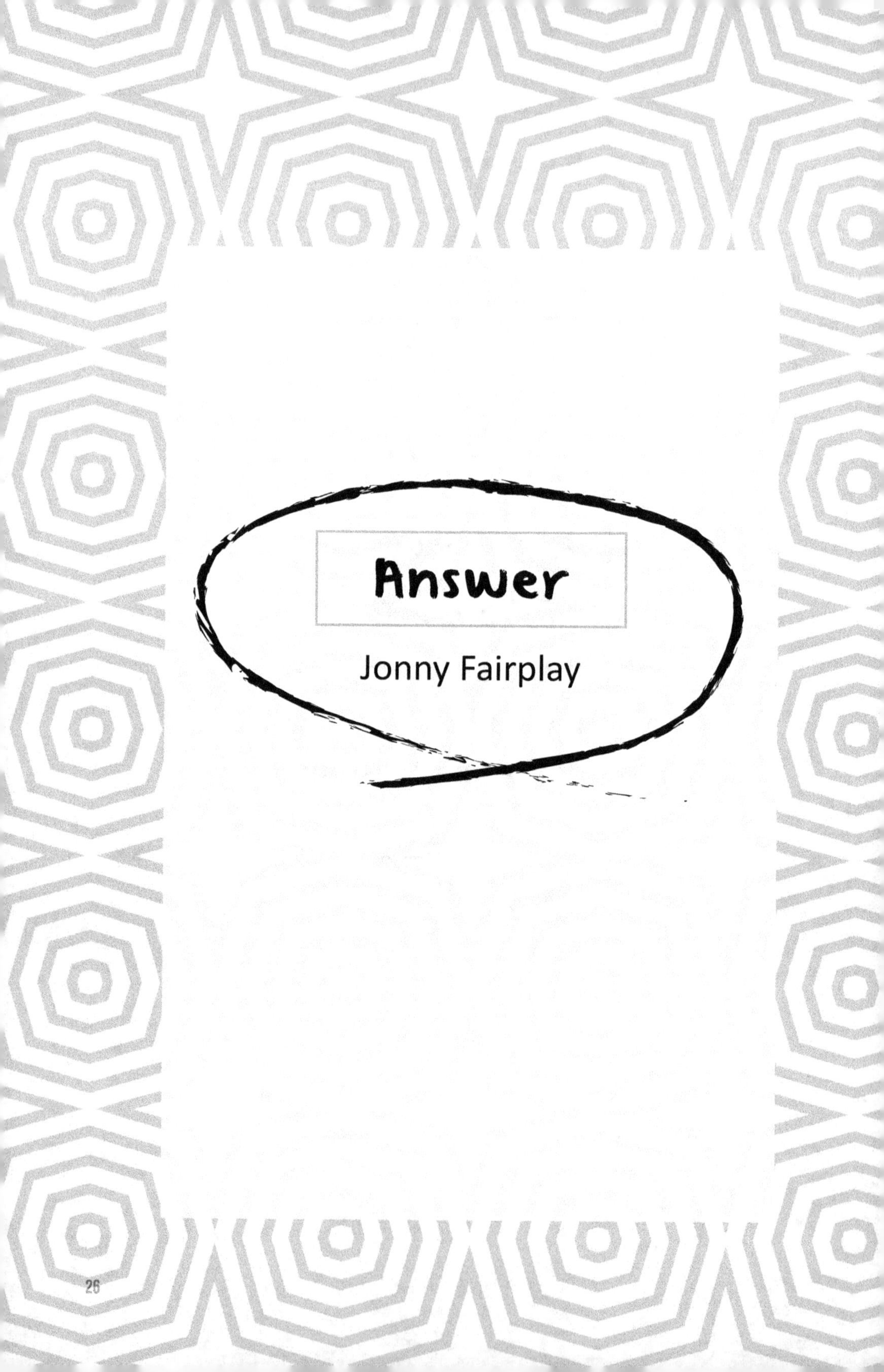

Answer

Jonny Fairplay

Question

Who was the first castaway
to leave the game without
being voted out?

Answer

Michael Skupin, who burned his hands in the campfire, was medically evacuated.

Question

Who won "Survivor: Palau" and is reportedly one of Jeff Probst's favorites of all time?

Answer

Tom Westman

BONUS

Round!

(Big chance to prove your "Survivor" love.)

BONUS Round!

You have 60 seconds to answer once the question is read aloud.
Through 46 seasons, 6 contestants have won individual
immunity five times in a single season. Name them.
(1 point for each name for a maximum of 6 points.)

Ozzy Lusth	Season 13, Cook Islands
Tom Westman	Season 10, Palau
Terry Deitz	Season 12, Panama-Exile Island
Colby Donaldson	Season 2, The Australian Outback
Mike Holloway	Season 30, Worlds Apart
Brad Culpepper	Season 34, Game Changers

Question

Who was the first-ever
unanimous winner?

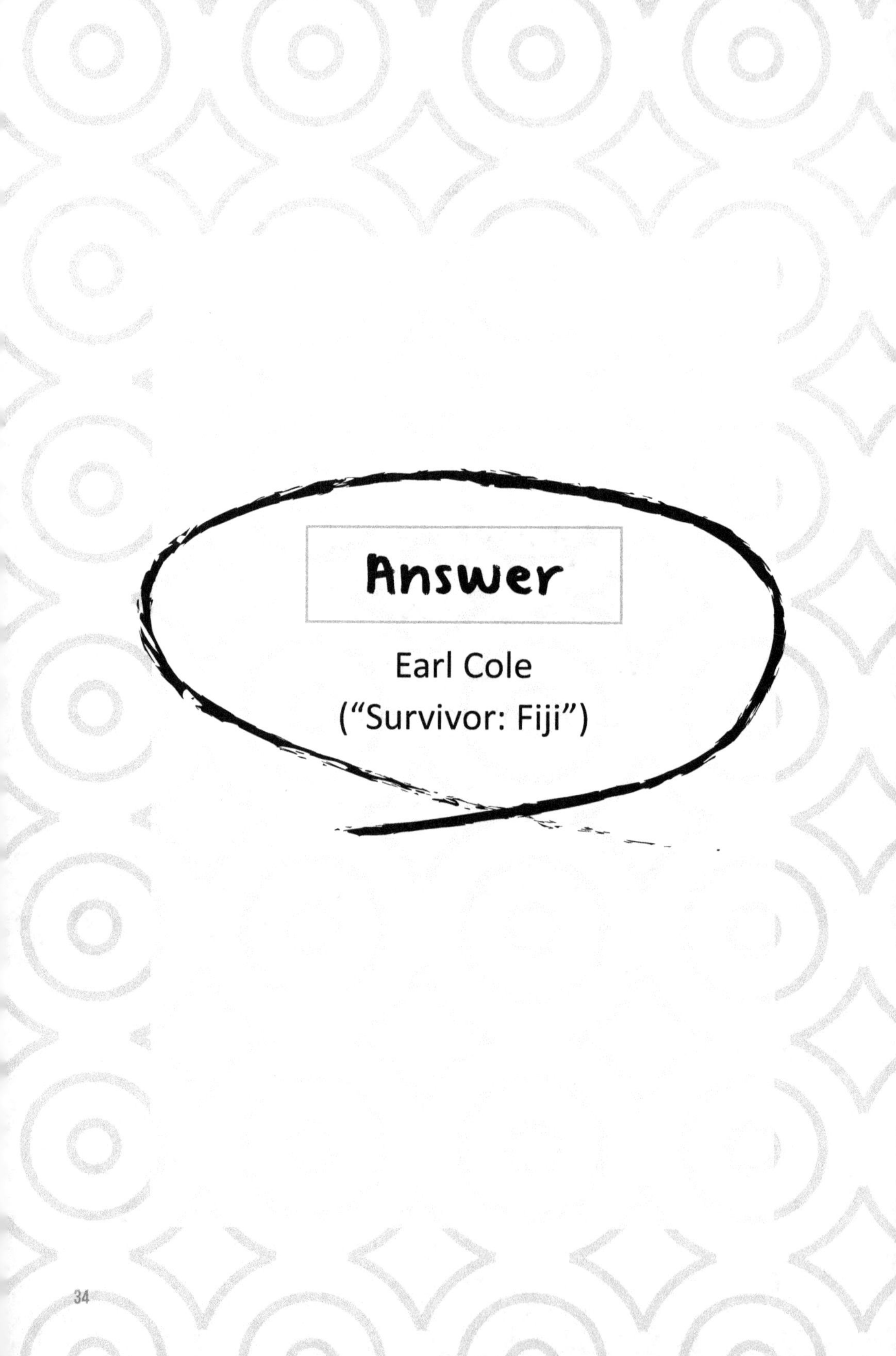

Answer
Earl Cole
("Survivor: Fiji")

Question

What winner played
in honor of his mother,
who was diagnosed with
lung cancer?

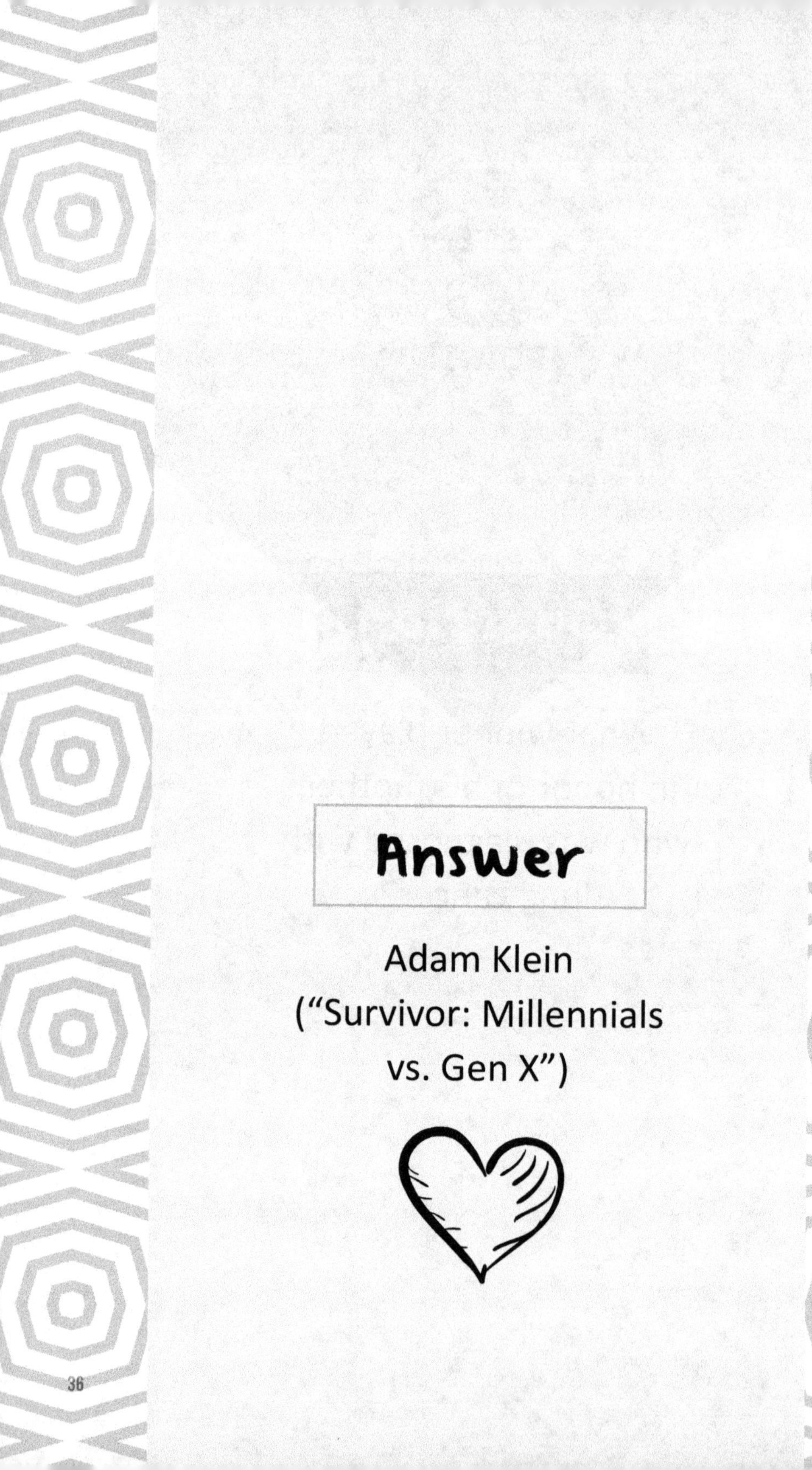

Answer

Adam Klein
("Survivor: Millennials
vs. Gen X")

Who won the second season of "Survivor" and never received a single elimination vote?

Answer

Tina Wesson

Question

What player attended
every single Tribal Council
during her season before
winning the game?

Answer
Denise Stapley

Question

Who is the only
Sole Survivor to play
multiple times and
never be voted out?

Answer

Jenna Morasca
(She won one time, and quit
the game another.)

Question

Who was the first person to be voted out of "Survivor" while in possession of not one, but two hidden immunity idols?

Answer

James Clement

2
POINTS
Question
Who was the first player
to win the game following
a tie vote at Tribal Council?

Answer

Wendell Holland

Question

What player finished
second to season 46 winner
Kenzie Petty?

Answer

Charlie Davis

Question

Who appeared on
"Survivor" three times
before winning the title?

Answer

Tyson Apostol

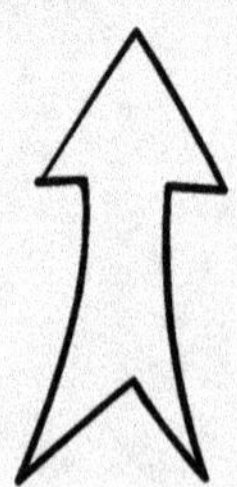

Question

How many people have won
"Survivor" three times?

Answer
None

BONUS Round!

(Outwit. Outplay. Outbonus.)

BONUS Round!

You have 60 seconds to answer once the question is read aloud. During season 42, Drea Wheeler was in possession of four advantages at one time. Name them. (1 point for each advantage named for a maximum of 4 points.)

An immunity idol
An extra vote
The Amulet advantage
The Knowledge is Power advantage

Question

What player wrote
a thesis paper on "Survivor"
before coming on the show
and eventually winning
season 26?

Answer

John Cochran

Most "Survivor" seasons last 39 days. Who had to play for 42 days in order to win her season?

Answer

Tina Wesson

Question

Several high-profile sports celebrities have played "Survivor," including Jimmy Johnson, John Rocker, and Jeff Kent. Which of those three lasted the longest in the game?

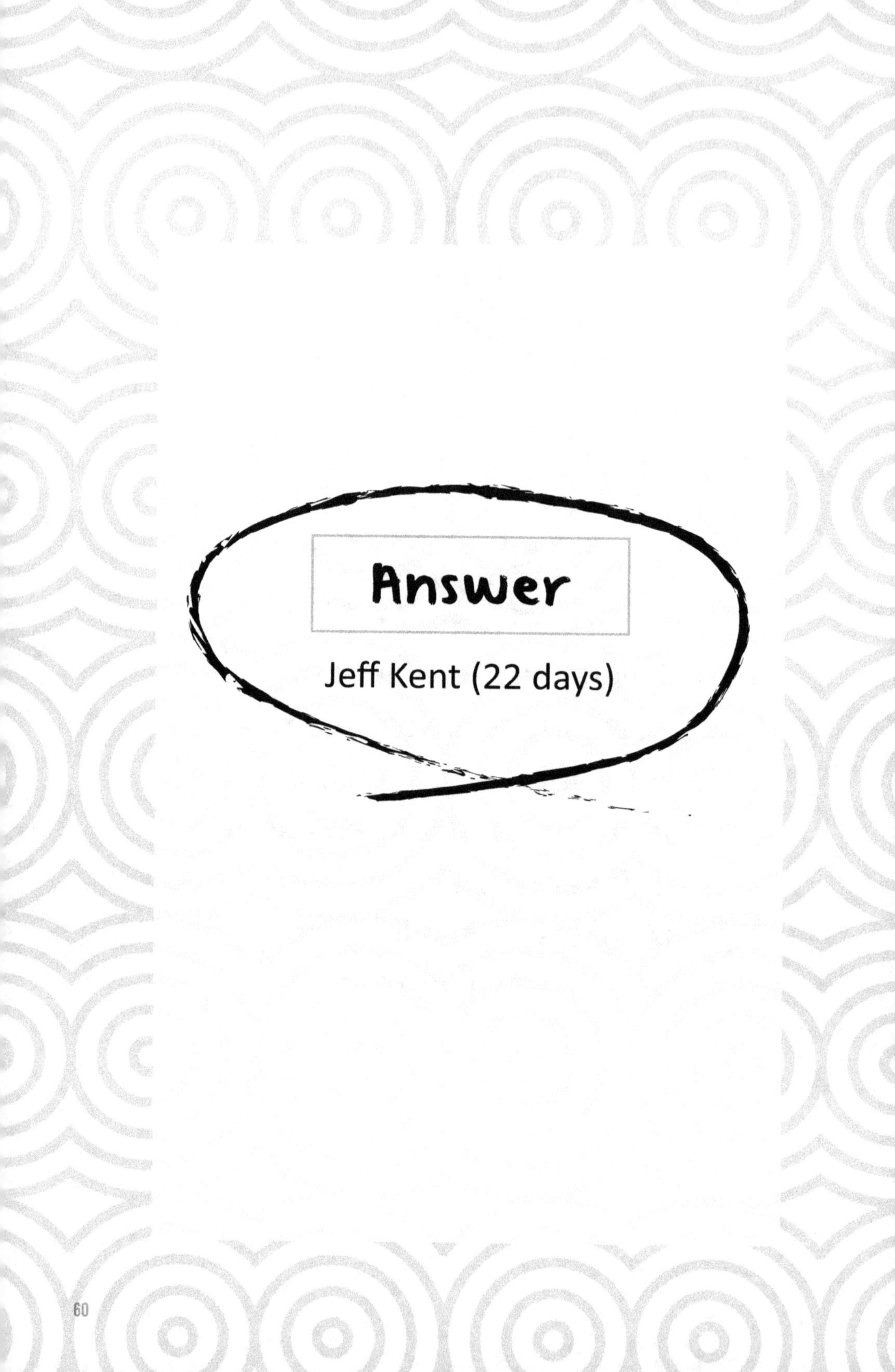
Answer
Jeff Kent (22 days)

Question

Who found herself alone on a tribe after her tribe lost eight consecutive immunity challenges before the merge?

Answer

Stephenie LaGrossa

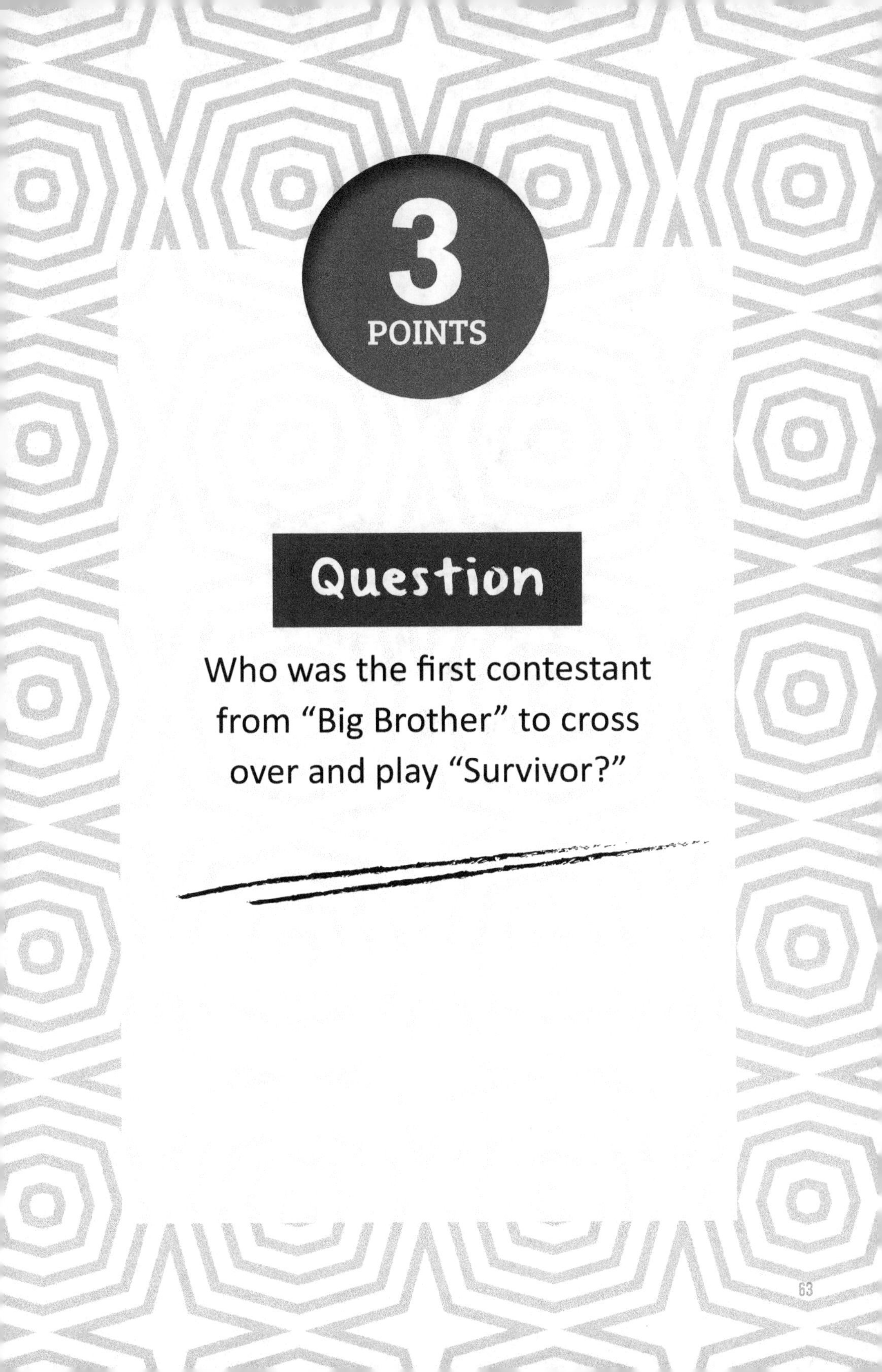

Question

Who was the first contestant from "Big Brother" to cross over and play "Survivor?"

Answer

Hayden Moss
(Winner of season 14
of "Big Brother")

Question

Multiple Choice:
What is the name of the
"Survivor" theme song?
A: New Horizons
B: Ancient Voices
C: Strongest Survivor
D: One World

Answer

B. Ancient Voices

BONUS

Round!

(Survivors ready?)

BONUS Round!

Who am I?

The three statements below apply to one specific "Survivor" contestant. You may take one guess after each statement is read.

Correct guess after one statement: 5 points
Correct guess after two statements: 4 points
Correct guess after three statements: 3 points

Statement 1: This contestant won a car without actually winning a challenge.
Statement 2: This contestant also competed on the reality show "The Amazing Race."
Statement 3: This contestant competed in three seasons total as of 2021 and won in the second appearance.

ANSWER: Amber (Brkich) Mariano

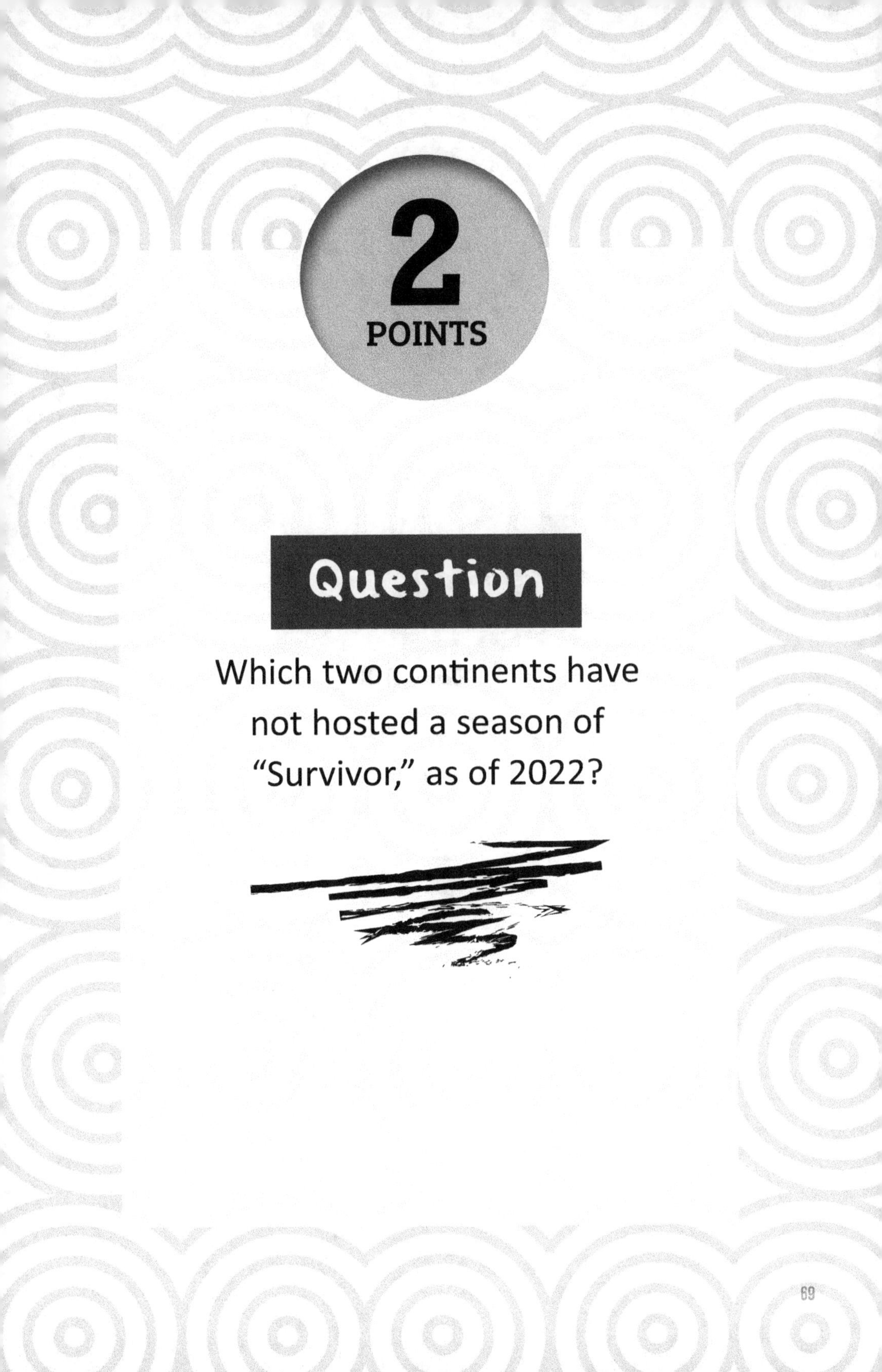

2
POINTS

Which two continents have not hosted a season of "Survivor," as of 2022?

Answer

Antarctica
and Europe

Question

Which Survivor gave away
his prize of a new truck as
part of an immunity deal,
only have the deal broken?

Answer

Yau-Man Chan

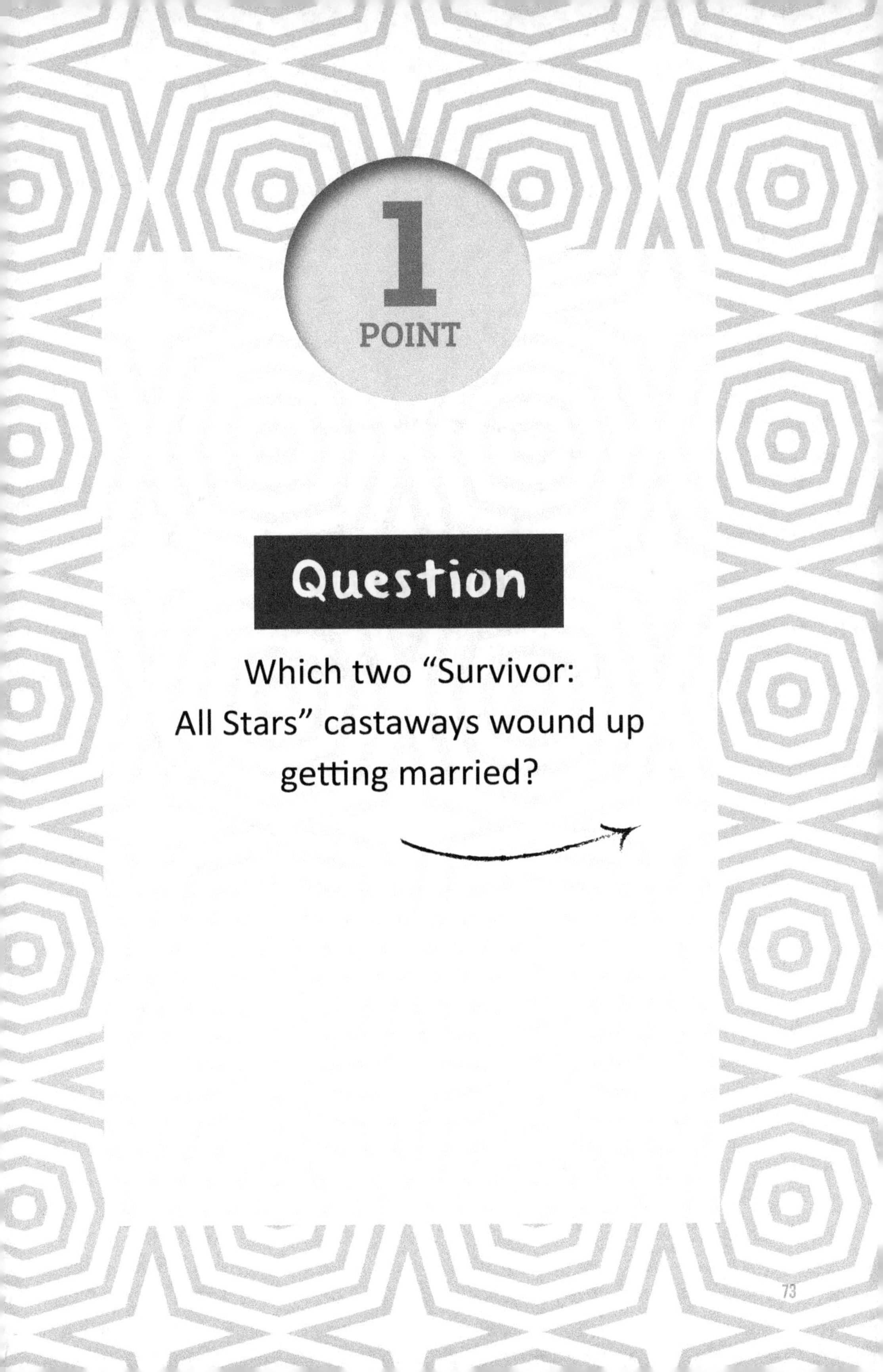

1
POINT

Question

Which two "Survivor:
All Stars" castaways wound up
getting married?

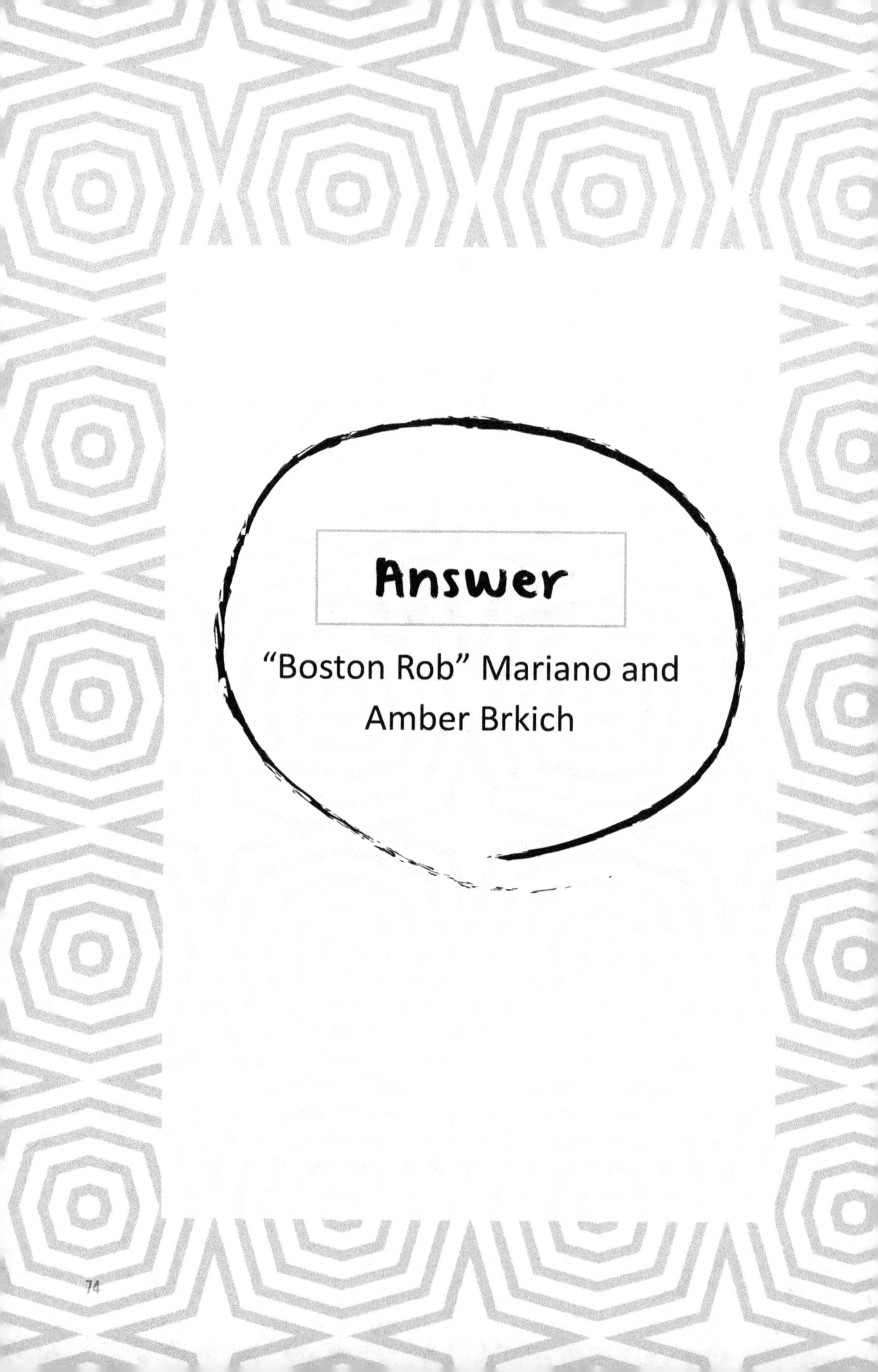

Answer
"Boston Rob" Mariano and Amber Brkich

Question

True or false: Yamil "Yam Yam" Arocho won season 44 in a unanimous vote.

Answer

False. He won seven of eight jury votes.

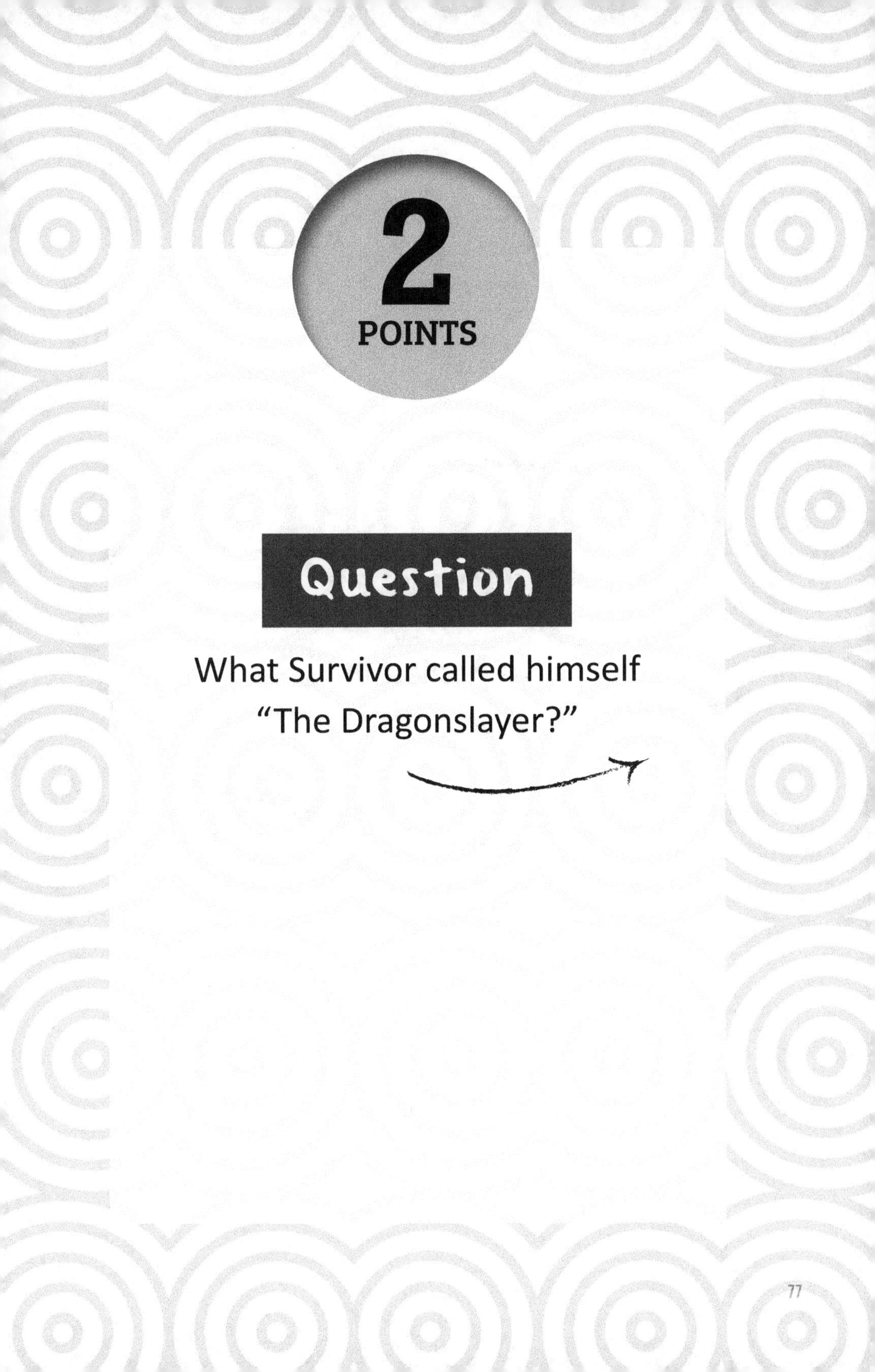

Question

What Survivor called himself
"The Dragonslayer?"

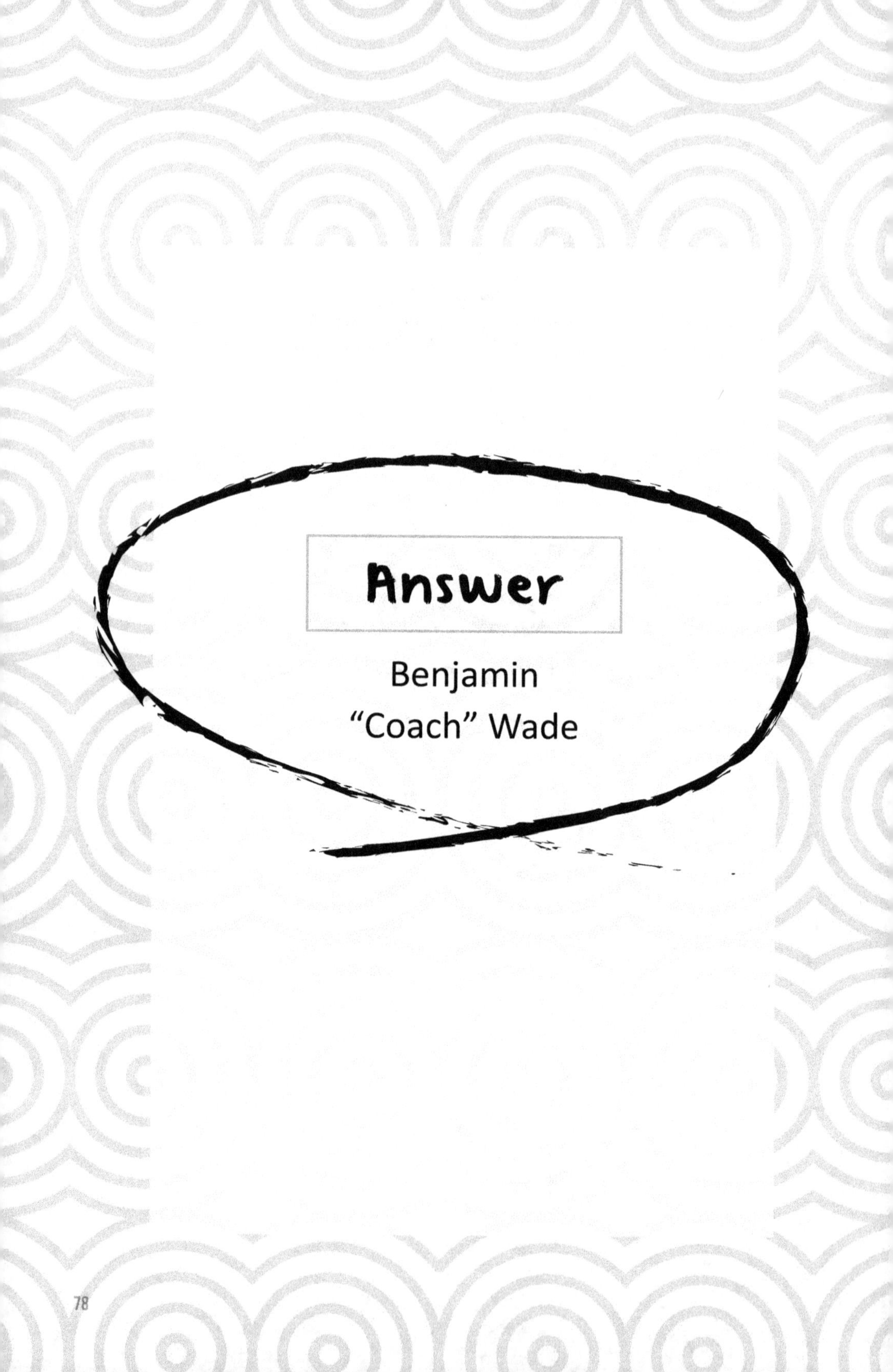

Answer
Benjamin
"Coach" Wade

What "Survivor" winner said he'd spend his winnings on "exotic expensive furs" for his shoulder, "jewels on these pretty fingers," and a "man tiara?"

Answer

Tyson Apostle

Question

Which castaway gave
his Hidden Immunity Idol
to a member of the
opposing tribe?

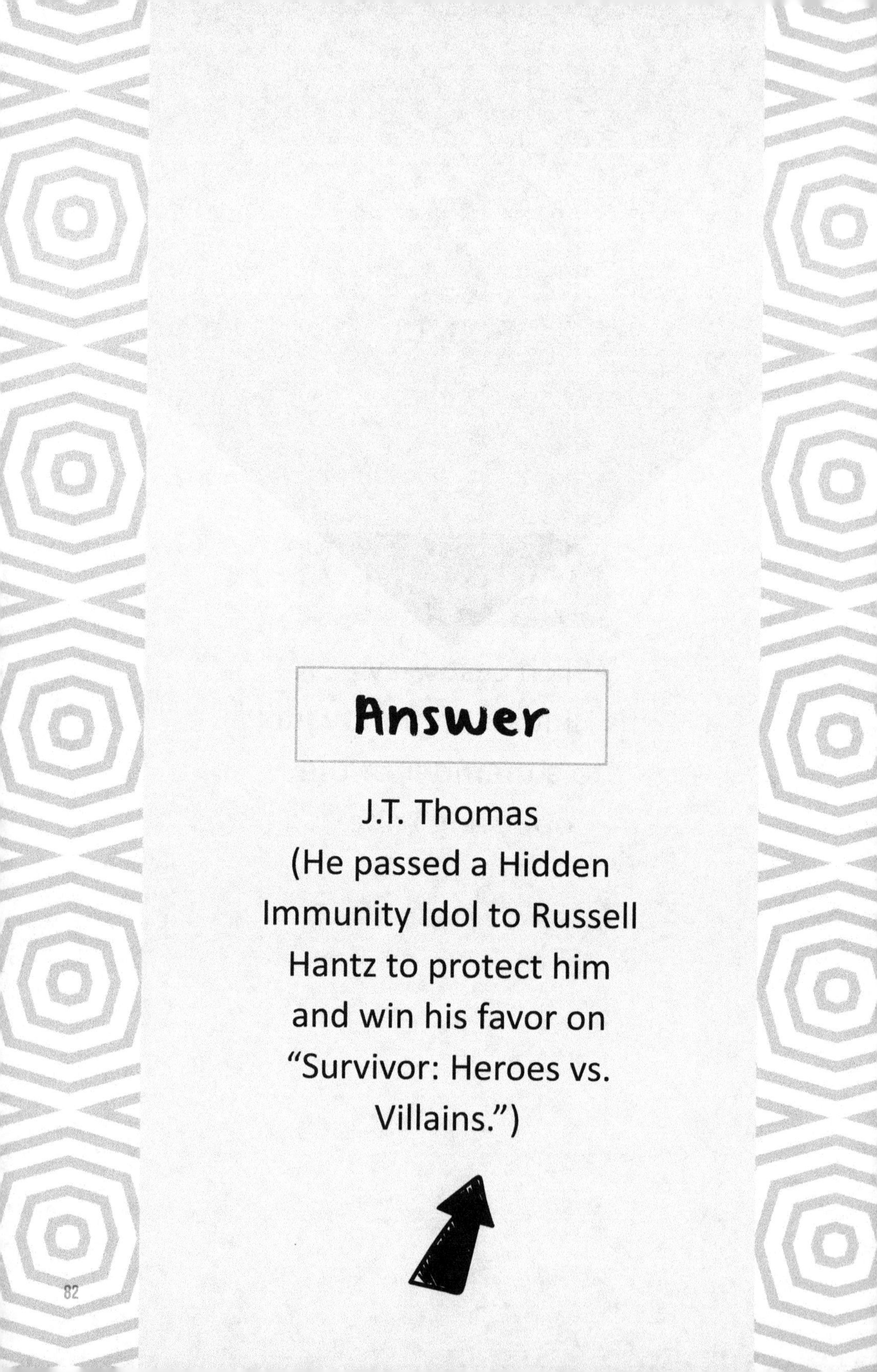

Answer

J.T. Thomas
(He passed a Hidden
Immunity Idol to Russell
Hantz to protect him
and win his favor on
"Survivor: Heroes vs.
Villains.")

Question

On how many
"Survivor" seasons has
Cirie Fields played
(through 2022)?

Answer
Four seasons

BONUS
Round!

(Don't let your torch get snuffed.)

BONUS Round!

You have 30 seconds to act out a Survivor contestant. You may use words as part of your performance. However, you cannot use the names of **any** specific contestant. If you successfully complete this task, you earn 4 points, and the person who guesses your character correctly earns 1 point.

Question

Multiple choice: Who has received the most career votes against them (36)?
A: Andrea Boehlke
B: Kelley Wentworth
C: "Boston Rob" Mariano
D: Ozzy Lusth

Answer

A. Andrea Boehlke

Question

In season 1, Sue Hawk gave
a famous Final Tribal Council
speech comparing the final
2 to what?

Answer

A snake and a rat

Question

Which season 2 contestant went on to co-host the talk show "The View"?

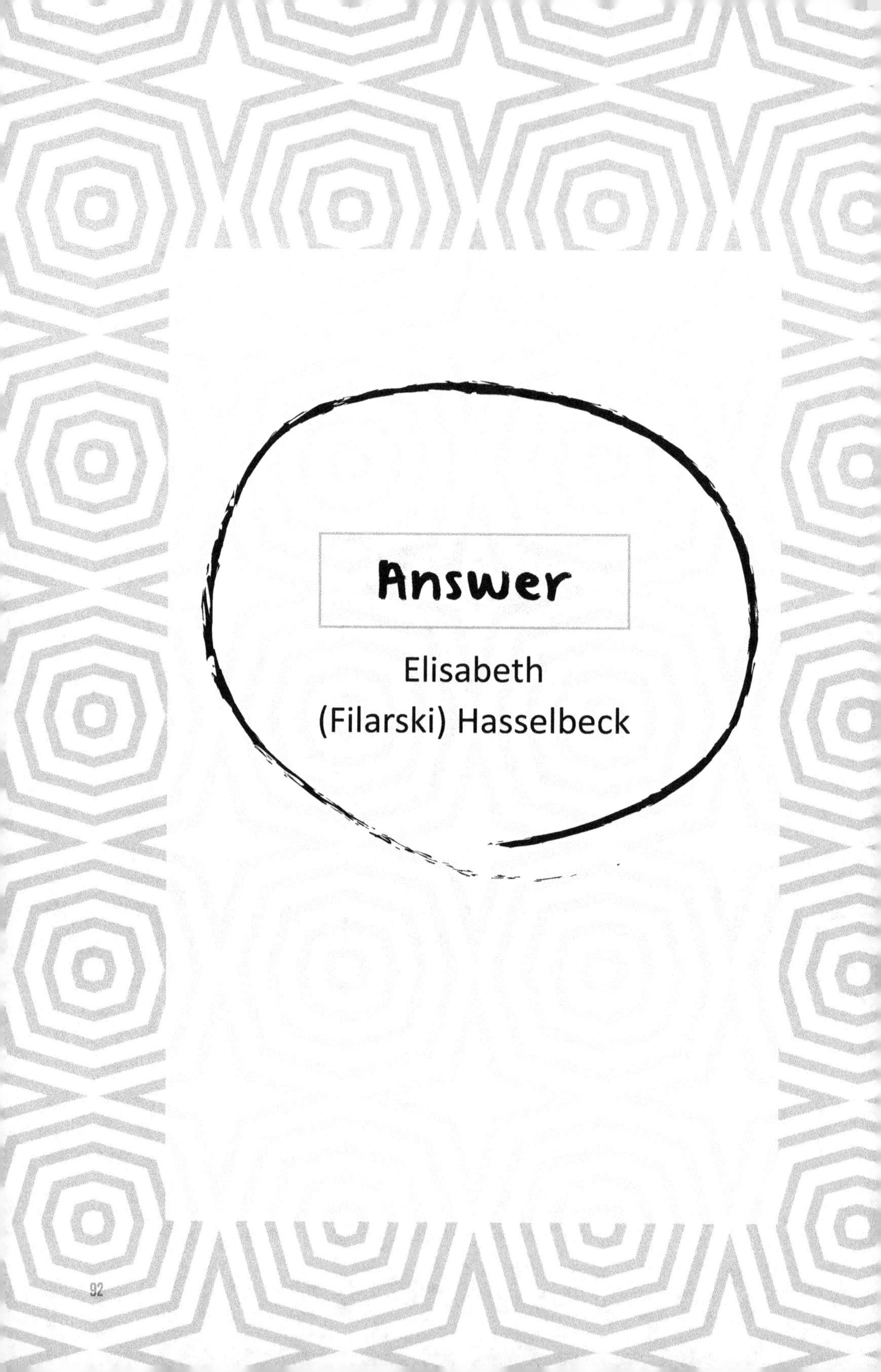

Answer
Elisabeth
(Filarski) Hasselbeck

Question

Who was the very first person ever voted out of "Survivor"?

Answer

Sonja Christopher

BONUS Round!

(Once again, the bonus round is back up for grabs.)

BONUS Round!

You have 60 seconds to answer once the question is read aloud. Through 42 seasons, 12 contestants have been chosen to NOT participate in a team challenge 6 or more times. Name as many as you can. (1 point for each name. You can only earn a maximum of 8 points.)

Sandra Diaz-Twine	13
Courtney Yates	12
Abi-Maria Gomes	8
Katie Gallagher	7
Cirie Fields	7
Janu Tornell	6
Caryn Groedel	6
Laura Morett	6
Monica Padilla	6
Shii Ann Huan	6
Corinne Kaplan	6
Parvati Shallow	6

Question

Parvati played two idols at the merge of "Survivor: Heroes vs. Villains" to protect tribemates Sandra and Jerri. Who went home instead?

Answer

J. T. Thomas

Question

In "Survivor: Worlds Apart,"
how were the tribes
determined initially?

Answer
By collar: White, Blue
and None.

Question

What does fire represent in the game of "Survivor?"

Answer

Life

Question

Which "Facts of Life" actress competed on "Survivor"?

Answer

Lisa Welchel

BONUS

Round!

(How bad do you want it?)

BONUS Round!

Who am I?

The three statements below apply to one specific "Survivor" contestant. You may take one guess after each statement is read.

Correct guess after one statement: 5 points
Correct guess after two statements: 4 points
Correct guess after three statements: 3 points

Statement 1: This contestant is the fifth player in series history to play in two or more seasons and never reach the jury phase.
Statement 2: This contestant left the game early with a medical emergency.
Statement 3: This contestant previously competed on the reality show "Big Brother."

ANSWER: Caleb Reynolds

Question

What "Survivor" winner said,
"People said you can't
play this game with emotion.
But look at me: Using
emotions as a weapon"?

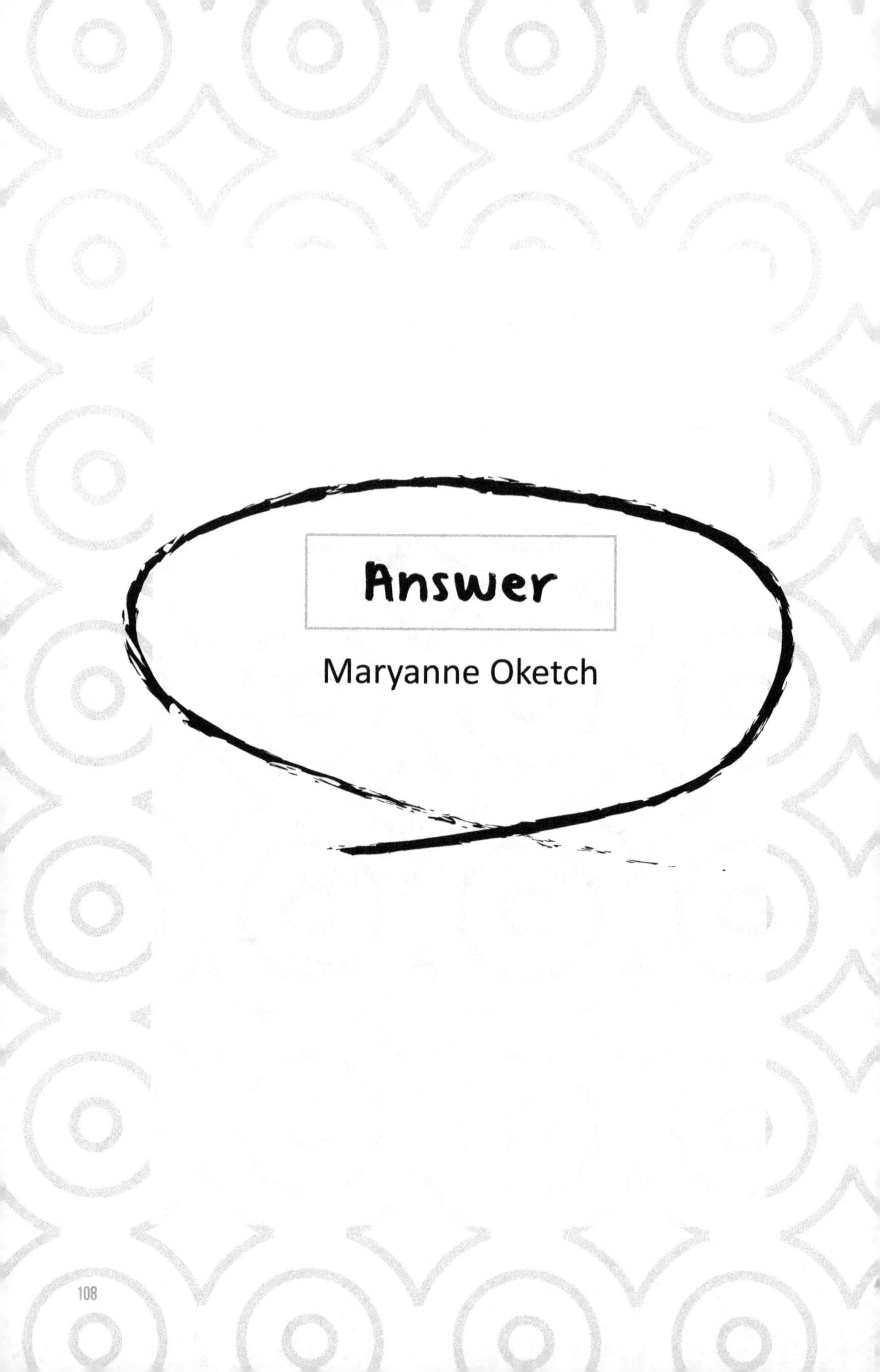

Answer

Maryanne Oketch

3

POINTS

Question

On "Survivor: Philippines," which player immediately bid all her money ($500) at a Survivor auction to win an advantage in the next immunity challenge?

Answer

Abi-Maria Gomes

What "Survivor" winner
went to jail for
failing to pay his taxes?

Answer

Richard Hatch (season 1)

Question

In season 1, which castaway used an alphabet strategy to decide who to vote out?

Answer

Sean Kenniff

BONUS

Round!

(The bonus round has spoken.)

BONUS Round!

You have 60 seconds to answer once the question is read aloud. Through 47 seasons, 15 seasons have had a Final 2 instead of a Final 3. Name as many runners-up as you can from these 15 season. (1 point for each name for a maximum of 8 points only.)

Kelly Wiglesworth	(Season 1, Borneo)
Colby Donaldson	(Season 2, The Australian Outback)
Kim Johnson	(Season 3, Africa)
Neleh Dennis	(Season 4, Marquesas)
Clay Jordan	(Season 5, Thailand)
Matthew von Ertfelda	(Season 6, The Amazon)
Lillian Morris	(Season 7, Pearl Islands)
Rob Mariano	(Season 8, All-Stars)
Twila Tanner	(Season 9, Vanuatu)
Katie Gallagher	(Season 10, Palau)
Stephenie LaGrossa	(Season 11, Guatemala)
Danielle DiLorenzo	(Season 12, Panama)
Amanda Kimmel	(Season 16, Micronesia)
Stephen Fishbach	(Season 18, Tocantins)
"Woo" Hwang	(Season 28, Cagayan)

True or false:

All "Survivor" contestants win money for playing.

Answer

True! The contestants win more based on how long they last, but even the first person voted out gets something.

Question

Multiple choice: How long was the longest "Survivor" challenge?

A: 8 hours 55 minutes

B: 9 hours 55 minutes

C: 10 hours 55 minutes

D: 11 hours 55 minutes

Answer

D. 11 hours 55 minutes
(Final immunity challenge
on "Survivor: Palau")

Question

What state has produced the
most "Survivor" contestants?

Answer
California

Question

How many total votes to win has Russell Hantz received during his appearances in Final Tribal Councils?

Answer

2 total. 2 in Samoa,
and 0 in Heroes vs. Villains

Question

Who won the final immunity challenge on the very first season of "Survivor?"

Answer

Kelly Wiglesworth

Question

True or False: More than 40 countries have a version of "Survivor" on TV.

Answer

True! 50 countries
and counting ...

BONUS
Round!

(Drop your buffs – it's a bonus round.)

BONUS Round!

You have 60 seconds to answer once the question is read aloud. Through 46 seasons, 11 players competed in two seasons in a row. Name as many as you can.
(1 point for each name for a maximum of 8 points.)

Rupert Boneham	(Pearl Islands, All-Stars)
Stephenie LaGrossa	(Palau, Guatemala)
Bobby Jon Drinkard	(Palau, Guatemala)
Amanda Kimmel	(China, Micronesia)
James Clement	(China, Micronesia)
Russell Hantz	(Samoa, Heroes vs. Villains)
Malcolm Freberg	(Philippines, Caramoan)
Joe Anglim	(Worlds Apart, Cambodia)
Shirin Oskooi	(Worlds Apart, Cambodia)
Michaela Bradshaw	(Millennials vs. Gen X, Game Changers)
Zeke Smith	(Millennials vs. Gen X, Game Changers)

Question

Who is the only Survivor to have been on both the Fans' tribe and the Favorites' tribe?

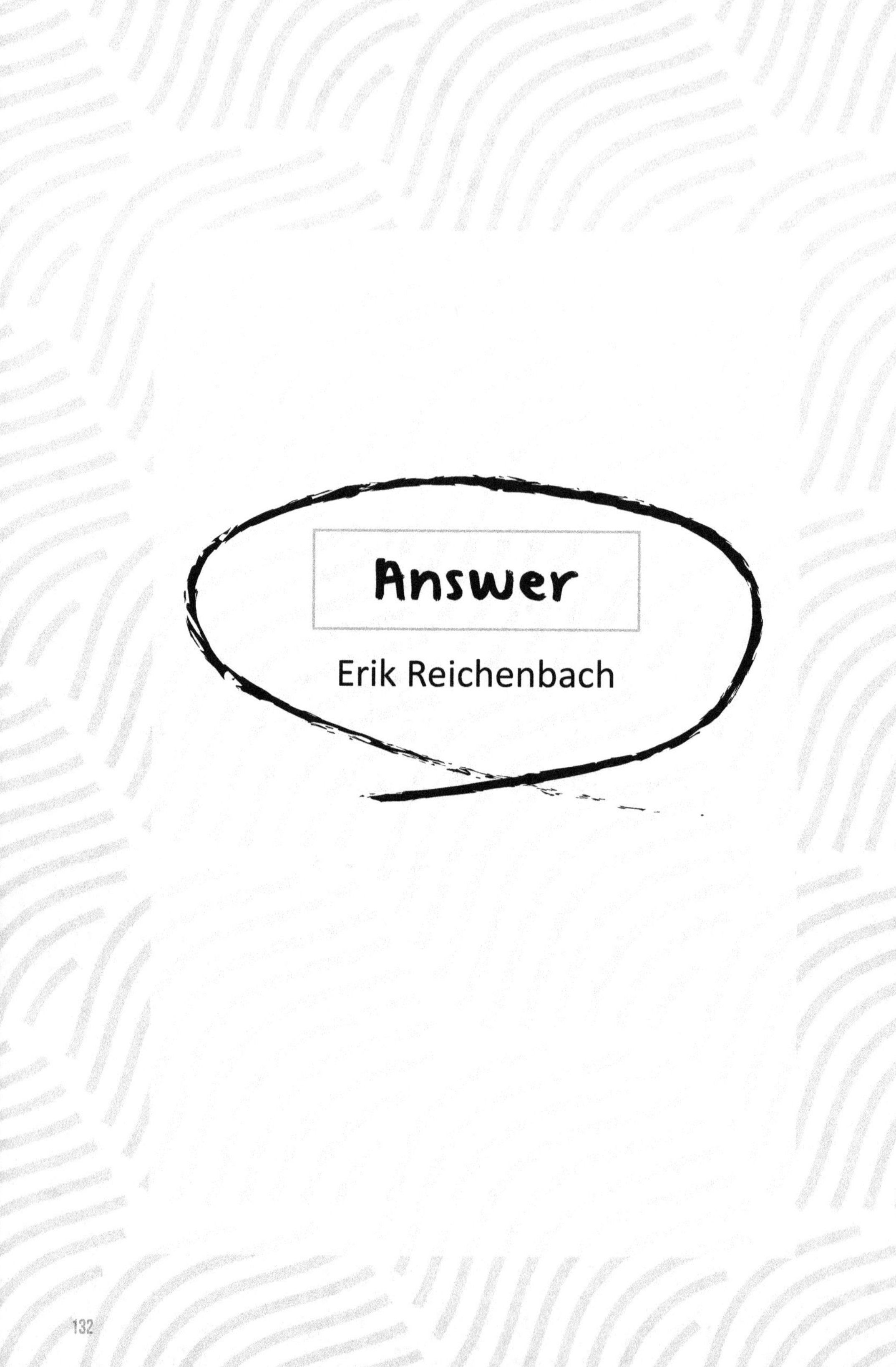
Answer
Erik Reichenbach

Question

How many of eight jury votes did Dianelys "Dee" Valladares get to win season 45?

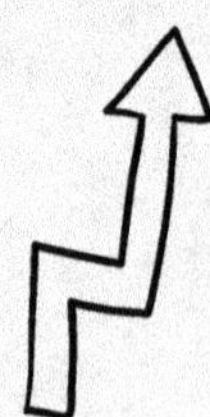

Question

In 2004, after filming on "Survivor: Vanuatu," Jeff Probst began dating a contestant. Who was she?

Answer

Julie Berry

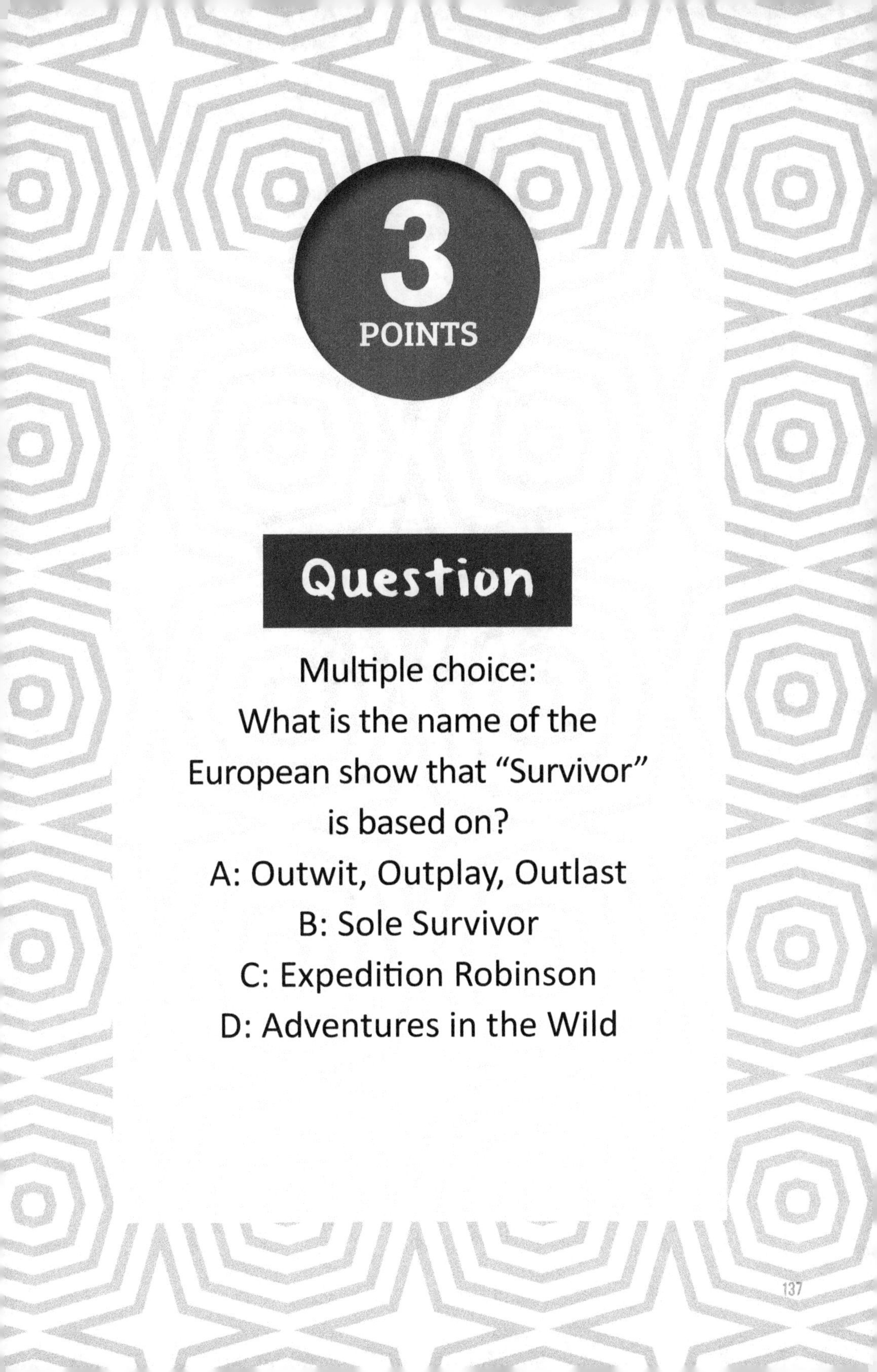

3
POINTS

Question

Multiple choice:
What is the name of the
European show that "Survivor"
is based on?
A: Outwit, Outplay, Outlast
B: Sole Survivor
C: Expedition Robinson
D: Adventures in the Wild

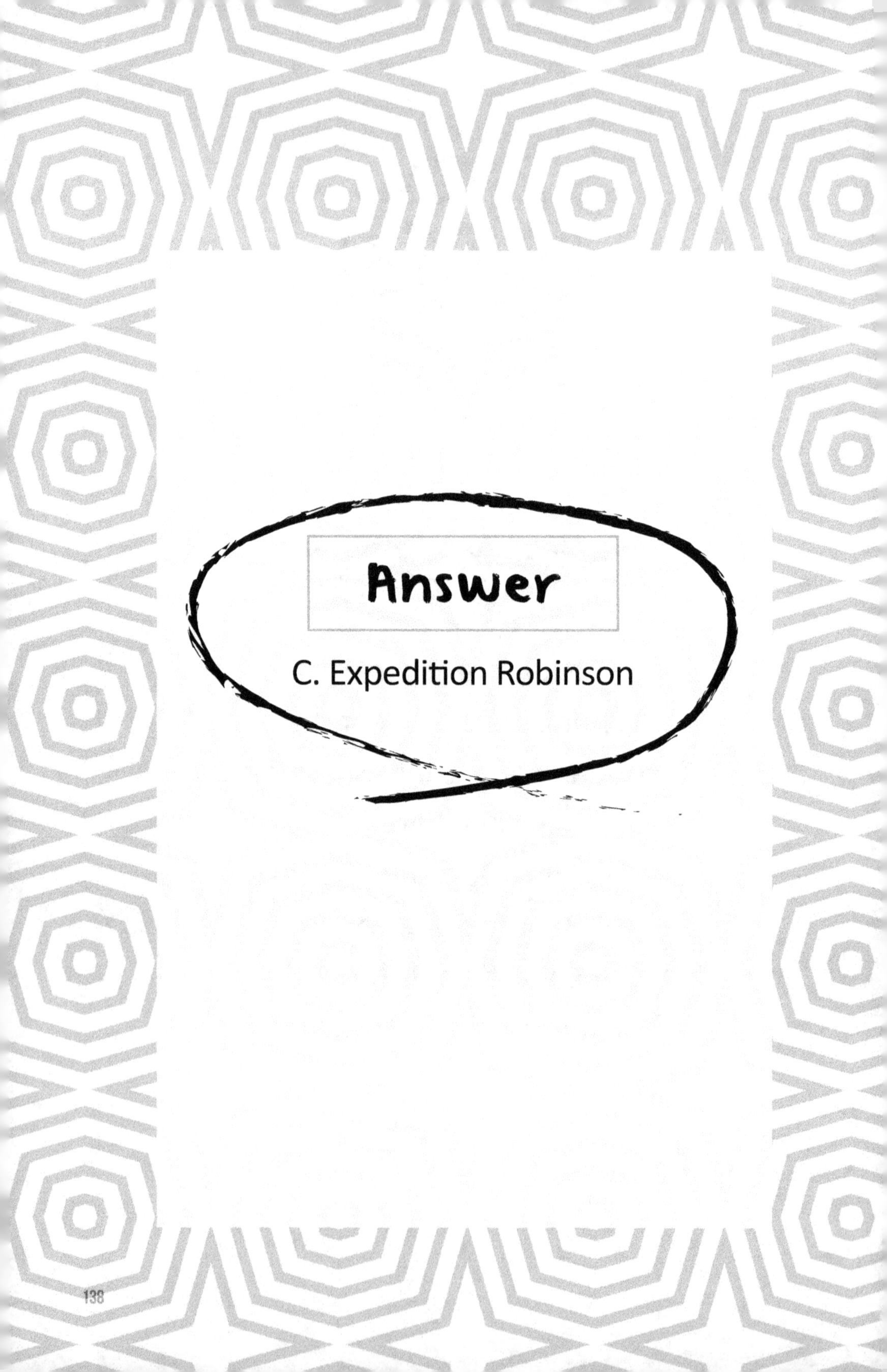

Answer

C. Expedition Robinson

Question

Who is the only castaway
to be voted out three times
in one season?

Question

What season was the first of the "Survivor New Era," where the game happens over fewer days at a faster pace?

Answer

Season 41

Question

Survivor 46 also holds the record for most consecutive people voted out while in possession of an idol. How many were voted out in a row?

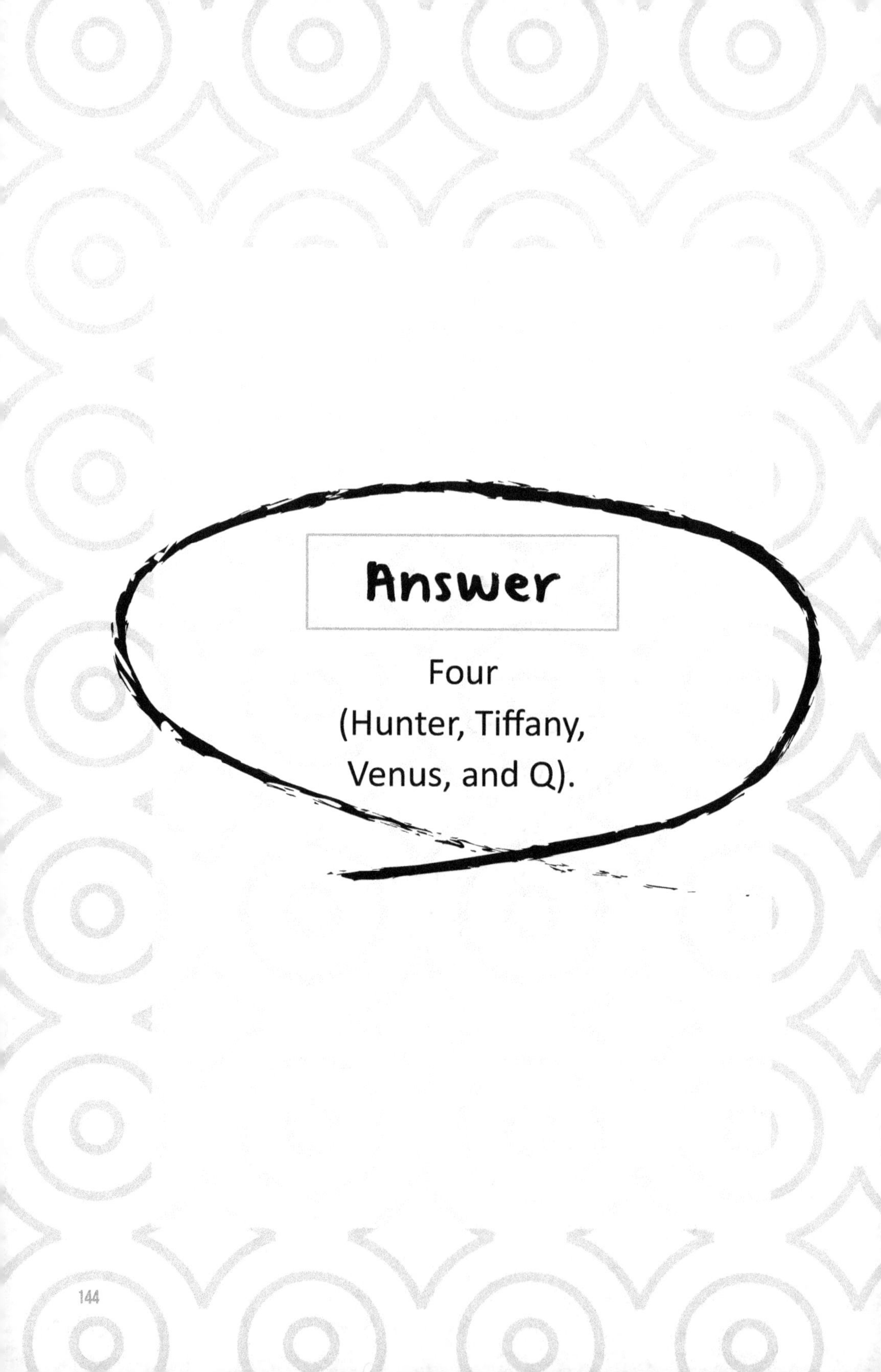

Answer

Four
(Hunter, Tiffany,
Venus, and Q).

Question

What "Survivor" player
is known for his tie-dyed
shirts?

Answer

Rupert Boneham

Who is the only competitor to appear on the show twice and get voted out first both times?

Answer

Francesca Hogi

Question

What is the
greatest number of
contestants medically
evacuated in one season?

Three
(Caleb Reynolds, Neal
Gottlieb and Joe Del Campo in
"Survivor: Kaôh Rōng")

BONUS

Round!

(For true "Survivor" fans only.)

BONUS Round!

You have 60 seconds to answer once the question is read aloud.
Through 46 seasons, 11 contestants have played the game of
Survivor for more than 100 days over multiple seasons.
Name as many as you can. (1 point for each name. You can
earn a maximum of 8 points.)

Rob Mariano	152 days
Parvati Shallow	149 days
Ozzy Lusth	128 days
Cirie Fields	121 days
Tyson Apostol	116.5 days
Aubry Bracco	111 days
Sandra Diaz-Twine	110 days
Amanda Kimmel	108 days
Amber Brkich	107 days
Rupert Boneham	104.5 days
Andrea Boehlke	103 days

Question

In the first 10 seasons of "Survivor," how many winners were women?

Answer

Five (Tina Wesson, Vecepia Towery, Jenna Morasca, Sandra Diaz-Twine and Amber Bkrich)

2
POINTS

Question

In what season was every
Final Three player
from New Jersey?

Answer

Season 40, Winners at War (Tony Vlachos, Natalie Anderson and Michele Fitzgerald.)

Question

How many seasons
were set in a cold, snowy
environment?

Answer
None

Question

What is the age of the youngest person to play "Survivor"?

18 (Will Wahl on Millennials
vs. Gen X)

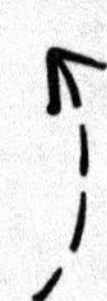

Question

Which "Survivor" player lied about being a firefighter who survived Hurricane Katrina, burned his teammates' socks, and emptied water canteens as part of an extreme psychological strategy?

Answer

Russell Hantz

2
POINTS

Question

Which season
of "Survivor" was the first to
feature an auction?

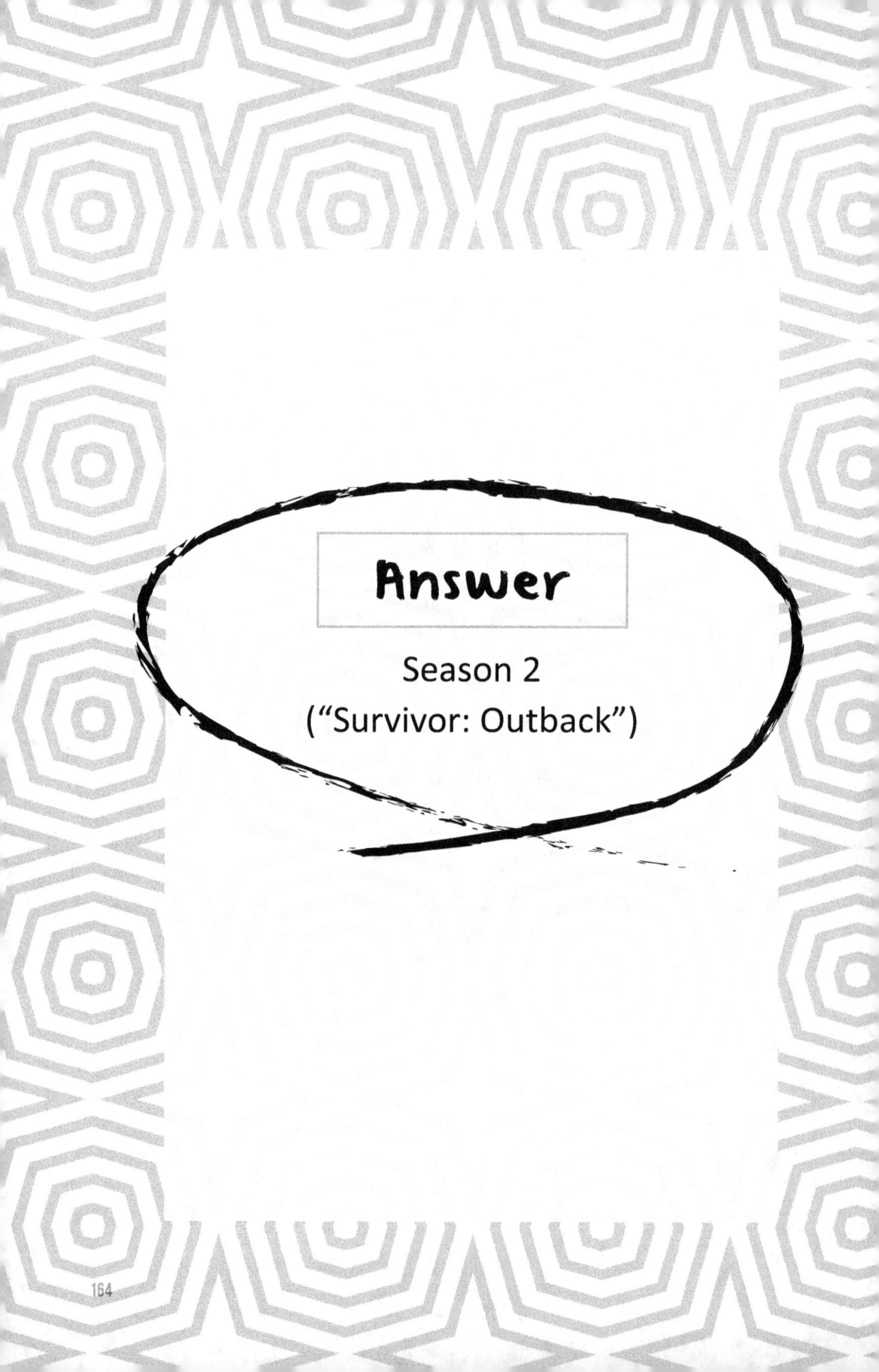
Answer
Season 2
("Survivor: Outback")

Question

What VH1 series did
Jeff Probst host before
"Survivor"?

Answer

"Rock & Roll
Jeopardy"

Which of the following has NOT been a factor in dividing tribes at the start of a season: age, gender, height, race, beauty.

Answer

The tribes have never been
divided by height.

BONUS

Round!

(Don't sit this one out.)

BONUS Round!

You have 60 seconds to answer once the question is read aloud.
Through 46 seasons, 10 contestants have won without receiving
a vote against them before reaching the Final Tribal Council.
Name as many as you can. (1 point for each name. You can earn
a maximum of 8 points.)

Tony Vlachos
Tina Wesson
Ethan Zohn
Brian Heidk
Sandra Diaz-Twine (first win)
Tom Westman
J.T. Thomas
John Cochran
Natalie Anderson
Nick Wilson

Question

How many players have the distinction of becoming the first member of the jury and the last member of the jury after competing in more than one season?

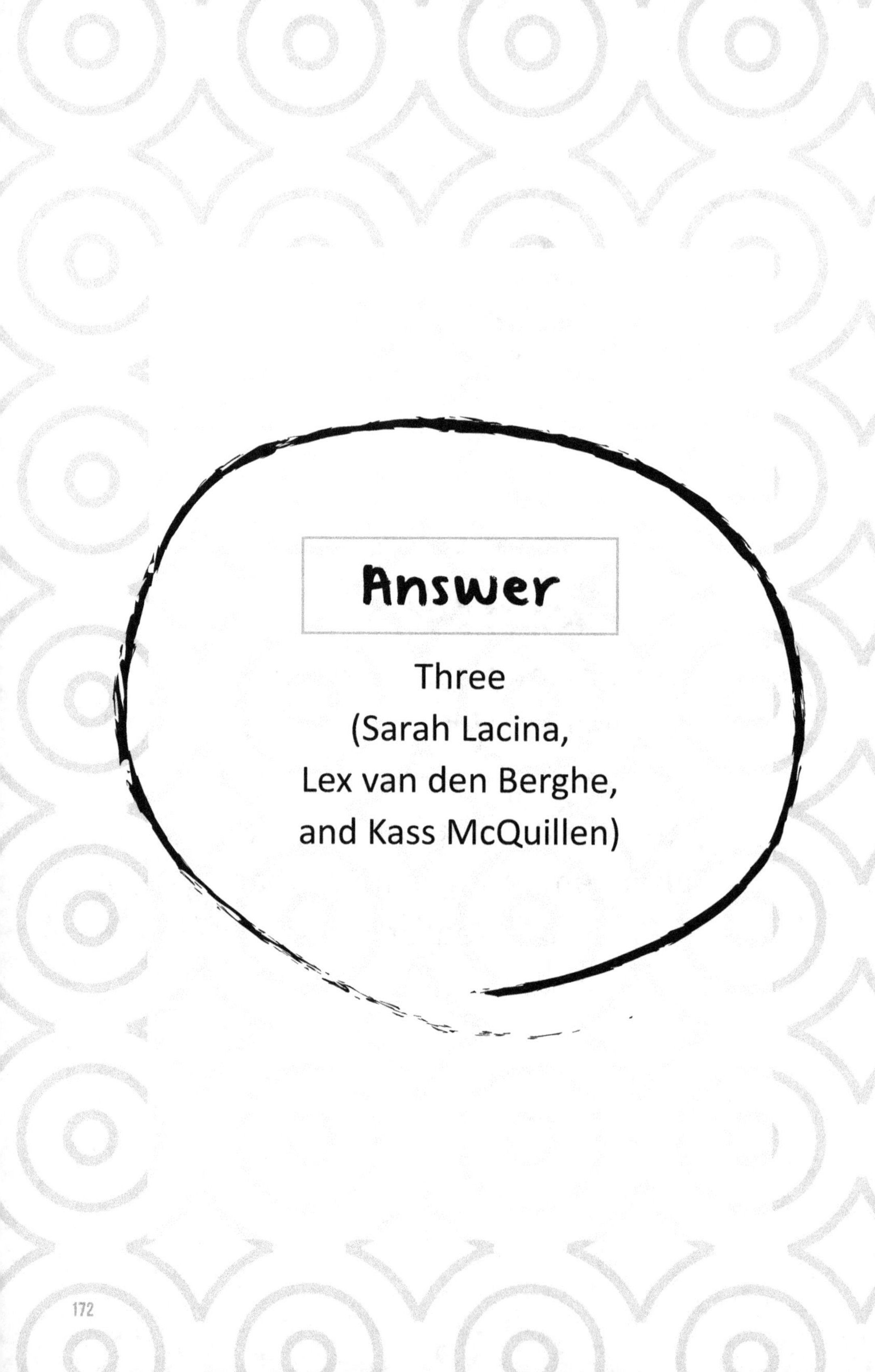
Answer

Three
(Sarah Lacina,
Lex van den Berghe,
and Kass McQuillen)

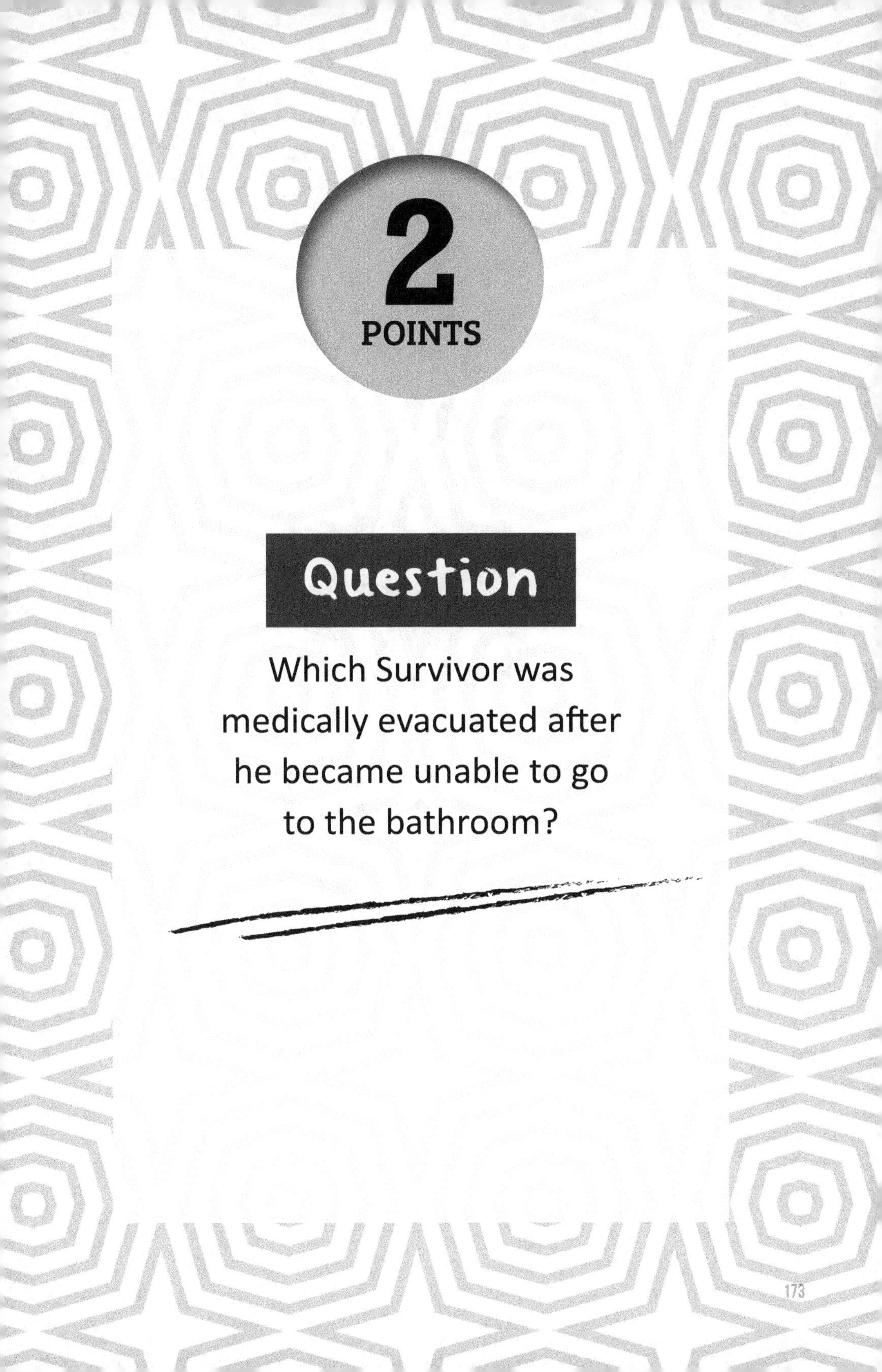

Question

Which Survivor was medically evacuated after he became unable to go to the bathroom?

Answer

Bruce Kanegai

Question

Tony Vlachos and Sarah
Lacina formed an alliance
using what name?

Answer

Cops R Us

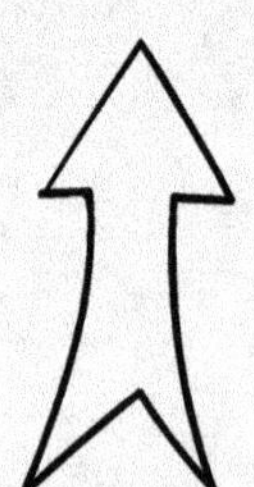

Question

What two players volunteered
to strip naked for cookies,
soda and peanut butter
as part of a challenge on
"Survivor: The Amazon?"

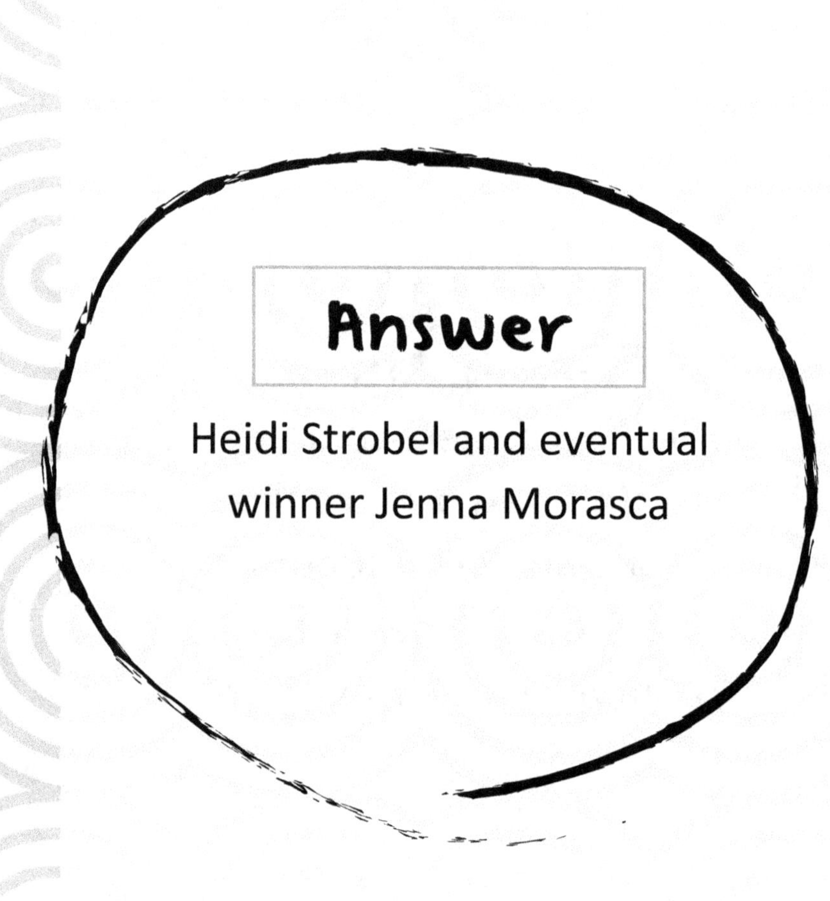

Answer

Heidi Strobel and eventual
winner Jenna Morasca

Which season of Survivor
was the first to feature
a Final Three?

Answer

Season 13 (Cook Islands)

Question

Who is the only Sole Survivor to never attend a pre-merge Tribal Council?

Answer

Michele Fitzgerald

Question

What season 40 (Winners at War) contestant hid in trees and other places to eavesdrop on other players' conversations?

Answer
Tony Vlachos

Question

On "Survivor: Micronesia,"
Erik Reichenbach gave up his
immunity necklace to prove his
loyalty to an all-female alliance,
who promptly voted him out.
What player accepted the
necklace from him?

Answer

Natalie Bolton

BONUS
Round!

(Only the strongest survive.)

BONUS Round!

You have 30 seconds to act out a Survivor contestant. You may use words as part of your performance. However, you cannot use the names of **any** specific contestant. If you successfully complete this task, you earn 4 points, and the person who guesses your character correctly earns 1 point. (Note: If you previously completed a charades task in this game, you must choose a different contestant this time.)

What contestant got revenge on Russell Hantz by throwing his favorite hat into the fire?

Answer

Sandra Diaz-Twine

Question

What player received no jury votes throughout the game, won the game in a unanimous decision, and won the Fan Favorite vote?

Answer

J. T. Thomas
("Survivor: Tocantins")

Question

Which Survivor season was
the first to have 90-minute
episodes?

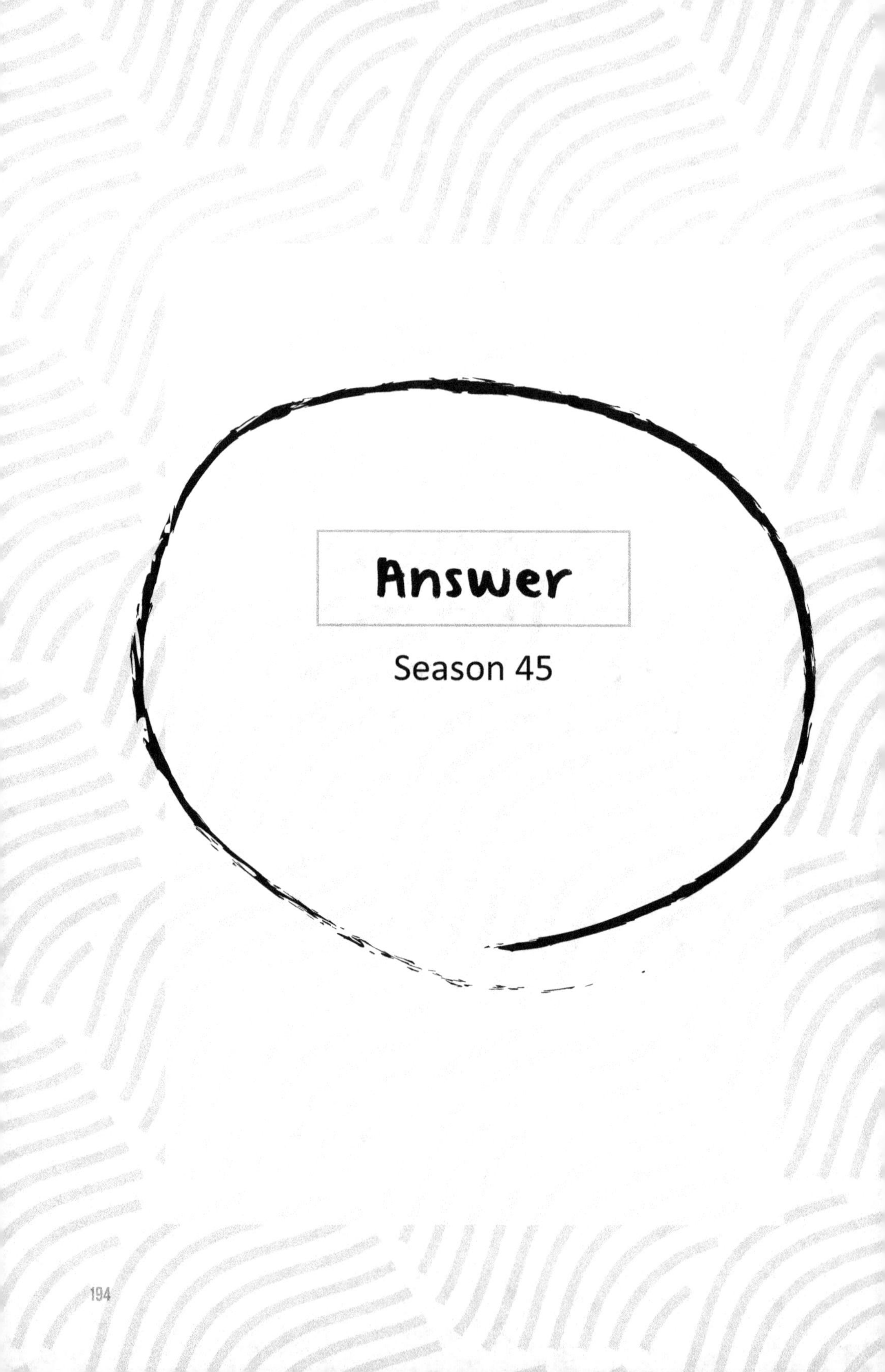

Answer

Season 45

Question

Who found a clue for a hidden
immunity idol and tossed it
into an active volcano?

Answer

Rob Mariano

Question

In season 40 (Winners at War), what new element was introduced that players could use to trade for luxury items or buy advantages during challenges?

Answer

Fire Tokens

Question

What player had the most
visits to Exile Island?

Answer

Sugar Kiper (5)

Question

Who is the first winner
from Canada?

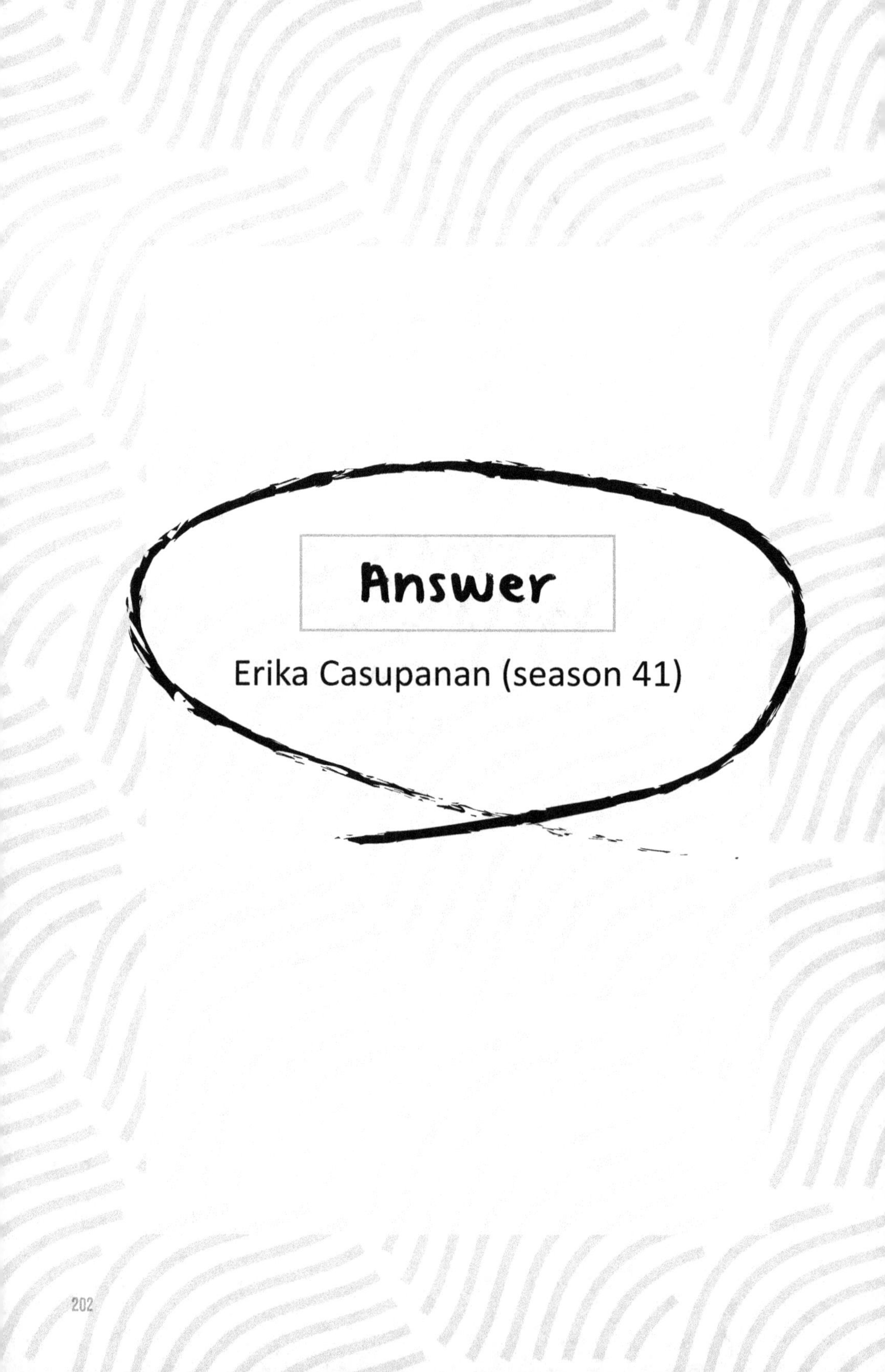

Answer
Erika Casupanan (season 41)

Question

Who is the first Survivor to successfully use a hidden immunity idol?

Answer

Mike Holloway

Thank you!

The purchase of this book supported
a small business owner. We hope you enjoyed it!

Questions? Comments? Please email jzbooksinfo@gmail.com.